St. Claret Centre

"Diane Crehan's book is full of first-person stories that remove the barrier between teacher and pupil. She helps the teacher get into the persona of the character whether it's Peter or Anna or Jonah, the cook at the household of Lazarus, Martha and Mary, and share in direct words the you-are-there happenings we call the Good News. This book, then, should be a welcome boon for teachers who want to engage children in the foundational stories of our faith by assuming the characters of those who first witnessed 'the wonderful works of God'."

William J. Bausch
Author, *A World of Stories for Preachers and Teachers*

"I like this book. The stories are so fascinating, I was tempted to read it straight through at one sitting. Instead, I made myself read each one as though I was hearing and savoring the telling of each story by Diane Crehan herself. She has done a wonderful job of taking familiar Bible stories and giving them fresh perspective through the point of view of different, compelling storyteller voices. She weaves magic through words that can be visualized, and thereby remembered, so they can be told again. Diane takes the tales of the Master Storyteller, gives each story its own flavor, its own character, its own uniqueness...and makes them come live again."

J.G. "Paw-Paw" Pinkerton
Stamford, CT
Founder of TELLABRATION, the Worldwide Evening of Storytelling

"Remembering, rendering, and dreaming are three essential ingredients to the complete life. Without them we diminish, even fade away! Diane Crehan has managed to capture these ingredients in her book, *Stories to Tell and How to Tell Them*. She has hit the nail on the head with her simple yet powerful instruction on storytelling. In a world where the acknowledgement of Christian practice is relegated to the privacy of one's home and church, out of the public forum, Crehan has provided the means for invigorating our ability to proudly tell the stories of faith.

"In a media deluged world where reality equates to visual perceptions, Diane Crehan has captured the medium, ever old but freshly new, for those who would tell the stories, all over again."

Msgr. Gregory M. Smith, Ed.D.
Director, The Institute for Religious Education and Pastoral Studies (REAPS)
Sacred Heart University, Fairfield, CT

"Diane Crehan is truly gifted in her ability to tell and teach with gospel stories. The Bible, of course, is more than anything a collection of stories. Jesus loved to tell them, as do all his greatest teachers and preachers. People sit up when they hear, 'Once upon a time...' Diane captures the best of this art. Her stories provide response, form bridges to the supernatural, inspire our hearts, and lift our souls."

Fr. Bill McCarthy
My Father's House, Moodus, CT

GW00778807

"For people of faith, it is the major preoccupation of the day: how are we to pass on the richness of the faith to the next generations? Diane Crehan provides both a compelling methodology—thoughtfully, carefully, and prayerfully prepared story-telling—as well as her own exciting and engaging narratives which quite effectively communicate the New Testament. Here are solid, creative tools for superb pastoral care and religious education for all ages. With this book, we have excellent assistance in the daunting task of passing on the faith. We should be encouraged!"

Stephen J. Sweeney, Ph.D.
President, The College of New Rochelle

"During Holy Week I was transported to another time and place while witnessing Diane Crehan, under the guise of Mary of Cleophas (Joseph's sister-in-law) tell her story. Diane vividly described Our Blessed Mother and the emotional turmoil she experienced during Christ's horrible sufferings. I was very impressed with her storytelling style of transmitting the gospel stories to an enraptured audience.

"How wonderful there is now a book available to teach others her storytelling method."

Pamela Brennan
Dalton, MA

"Diane Crehan has a gift. She has the ability to tell a story and create the impression in your mind that you were there at that specific moment, hearing the story for the first time from an eyewitness. These stories remind us that these events, just like our faith, are just as real and important in our daily lives as they were to the people who experienced them 2000 years ago."

Mark Dennen
Newtown, CT

I Remember Jesus

Stories to Tell and How to Tell Them

DIANE CREHAN

XXIII

TWENTY-THIRD PUBLICATIONS

Mystic, CT 06355

Dedication

For Patrick, who heard the stories of Jesus
and who knows the Jesus of the stories

Twenty-Third Publications
185 Willow Street
P.O. Box 180
Mystic, CT 06355
(860) 536-2611
(800) 321-0411

ISBN: 0-89622-981-5
Library of Congress Catalog Card Number: 99-71174
Printed in the U.S.A.

Table of Contents

More Miracles in Galilee

Later Days in Judea

The Last Days

The Promise Fulfilled

Three Additional Stories

Introduction

A little boy stopped me in the hallway of the grammar school where I had come to tell multicultural stories. He looked up and said in a whisper, "You're the lady from church that tells stories about…Jesus." I smiled, but I felt like one of the early Christians forced to share faith secretly. And I felt a crush of sadness for this boy and for all the other children growing up in our post-Christian era. He had remembered me from the stories I'd told at children's Masses, but it was clear that such stories were not told here. They were secret stories told only in the safety of a church. Long gone from schools like this are the wooden plaques with the Ten Commandments, the daily Our Father, the Christmas pageant with the hymns that were part of every public school assembly until the 1960s. T.V. families are now the role models, but they don't pray or go to church. In fact, in the world of television, Christianity is noteworthy for its absence.

Children today hear little if anything Christian, apart from the time they spend in religion class and the hour they spend at Mass. Parents and catechists compete with a world that is creature-centered and temporal, yet our belief is God-centered and eternal. Without the moral code and common belief that were nearly universal in the first half of this century, we must clear the lot, dig the rocky ground, and pour the footings. We have to build the foundation for a house of faith.

This book of stories is intended to help you build that foundation and in the process find a new direction in teaching. It's not a new idea. Storytelling is the world's oldest form of communication, but it's still the best way to teach. A story that's alive and vivid captures the "child" of any age and stays in the memory like an old friend, always ready for a return visit. A story can grow, as one chapter is added to another and characters become individual and discernible. We come to know how they will act; we come to know who they are. In this age of information overload, surrounded as we are by global facts, a story can also bring peace and order. The group gathers around to listen: "It happened, one day…" and teller and listener travel together as the story unfolds.

God spoke to the Chosen People in signs and symbols, dreams and visions, as well as through words. Abraham heard the voice of God and was visited by angels. Moses saw flames that couldn't consume a desert bush. Quail fell from the heavens when the Israelites begged for meat. The walls of Jericho fell. Hailstones beat down on the Canaanites and the river overflowed when Deborah ordered her soldiers to fight. God also spoke to the Chosen People through prophets who wrote down words of promise and words of warning.

Who could forget such God-filled happenings? The Israelites remembered days of glory and days of exile. They knew the Lord had called them, led them, and remained with them, even when they failed to obey his commands. The inspired Hebrew writers did not formulate creeds and doctrines; they just wrote down the story. And the story was told over and over through the long years of waiting for the promised Savior.

Somewhere along the way in our tradition, we seem to have focused our teaching on creeds, formulas, and doctrines, instead of the ongoing story of God's great care for his people. God did send his Son to live in our midst and his saving sacrifice is the heart of what we believe. We still need to teach our creeds and doctrines; they are part of our church heritage. But since we have only so much time to teach, to prepare young children for the sacraments, and to give them the basis for a lifelong faith, let's first tell the story!

We are all storytellers. We tell our own story, our family stories, our nightmare vacation stories, rescue stories, birthing stories, stories of triumph or sorrow. To our soul-friends we tell our faith story. When we have a good story to share, we often use the same words, pause at the same place, and watch the expressions on the faces of our listeners. We can remember every detail of the day we arrived at summer camp, the day we were accepted at college, or when a stranger appeared to help us when we were stranded on the roadside. Weddings, anniversaries, births, and deaths remain with us in story.

The goal of this book is to make some of the New Testament stories as familiar as our own stories and to show even the most reluctant parent or teacher how to tell them. There's something that happens when you start a story. The audience is transported. Truly. In just a few minutes they are quite literally taken away from the church pews, the chalkboard-lined room, or the circle of chairs. A wonderful silence descends and spreads. Whole congregations of listeners stop coughing, children stop fidgeting. A holy peace seems to enter a place when a story begins. The first few times I told stories at family Masses I was frightened by the silence. It seemed as if the people weren't breathing! That's the power of story to connect with the imagination, the deep wonderful space where time and place are suspended. No one seems to need to leave the church or the classroom in the middle of a story.

Who doesn't want a Sunday homily, a religion class, or a family evening to be an adventure, an experience, a mystical journey to a far-off place? And something even greater can happen when we use story to share the message of Christ. Storytelling can give LIFE to the life of Christ.

"But, we read the Bible stories," teachers tell me.

"It's not the same," I respond. The book comes between the reader and the listeners. The book owns the message and the reader is more like an announcer. You can't see the children's faces when you're reading from a book. When a story is told, every furrowed brow or delighted smile puts the teller in contact with the deep thoughts of the children. Tellers *have* the story like a great gift to be given in joy to those who are gathered. When a story is told, the teller speaks from personal knowledge, and instead of an illustration in a book, the listener forms his or her own full color image of the spoken words. One student wrote: "I like it that you make a picture in my head." For some children it is a startling new reality: mental pictures of people and places that come into their heads as the story is told. They bring to life the people of the Book: a young girl meeting an angel; a faithful old man in the temple holding the child Jesus; fishermen in a storm; the glorified Jesus on Tabor.

I have also found that most children can repeat a told story, and it's wonderful to let them. Some will use the gestures they saw the teller use or the inflection used at a dramatic moment. Others will give their own unique interpretation while essentially repeating the story. And isn't that the point?

I first experienced the power of storytelling when I told stories from different cultures to public school students in the primary grades (children like the boy in the school hallway). I used various accents and chose stories that were humorous but had a message. In each session, the thirty minutes flew by and we didn't know how it could be time to stop. When I received their illustrated letters in the mail, I knew they had thoroughly enjoyed the experience, that they had comprehended the stories and had gotten the message. They were effusive in their thanks and insightful in their reflections. Their drawings were detailed with balloons over the characters quoting specific words I had used.

I knew then, there was power in telling stories and I added marvelous Br'er Rabbit stories to my repertoire, especially those that included Christian themes. One school regularly scheduled me in March, and since I have a penchant for the Irish anyway, I learned a number of Irish stories. Many included "the little people." It was when one group of children reported to their parents that they had actually seen the leprechauns on the stage, that I decided it would be best to tell more life-changing stories.

My friend Kathy was the DRE at our parish at the time. She was desperate for a way to help students who were preparing for confirmation to come to know and really understand the Holy Spirit. Could you tell them a story? she asked. These many years later I can still remember the terror I felt as I walked in to face the ninety teenagers sitting on the floor in the lecture room. I brought a folded letter. I said it was from Peter, and that he wanted me to tell his story in his own words. It was my outline, not that I could look at it, but it gave me courage to know I had something written down.

"I was a great fisherman," Peter began, "my brother Andrew and I kept our boats in Capernaum, on the western shore of a lake we called a Sea." The room grew still. For fifty minutes no one moved. Peter, the fisherman, took them on a journey through the life of Jesus from a miraculous catch of fish to the Spirit's descent. He told them how he was changed when the Holy Spirit came with power. At the end "Peter" challenged the students to be open to all the gifts the Holy Spirit had to give them.

The story was well received, and so began an adventure I wish for all of you that read this book. The following section will show you how easy it is to learn and tell Bible stories. You may have butterflies at first, even feel terror on occasion, but if you carry on, you will find the most wonderful sense of joy from introducing children to the Jesus who said: "Let the little children come to me, forbid them not, for to such belongs the kingdom of God."

We know Jesus was a magnificent storyteller. Crowds sat for hours on the gentle slope of a hill listening to him talk of sowing seed and finding treasures in fields, of wayward sons and good Samaritans. He used stories to explain the Kingdom of God and stories to show people how to live. He also lived a story: healing the sick, forgiving sinners, following after lost sheep. He suffered and died and rose from the dead, just as he said he would. After Jesus said his last goodbye from the top of Mount Olivet, the disciples continued to meet for the breaking of the bread and they told stories to keep his memory alive. Like family stories told around the hearth or on the back porch, at birthdays or on Christmas night, they laughed and cried as they remembered him.

When the Holy Spirit came, they were baptized with fire, empowered, filled with grace, and they went out to tell the story to the world. Each generation heard the story from the generation before, and so the Christian faith came to us through storytelling, before it was ever written down.

But where do we start with a testament full of words? For this book I have chosen stories that will introduce the children to Jesus in his own time and place and give an overview of his life, death, and resurrection. There are the early stories of expectation, birth, flight, delay at the temple, and then the stories from Jesus' public life that are the most essential for children in sacramental years. I have included several miracle stories, Holy Week stories, the resurrection, ascension, and the coming of the Holy Spirit. In all of the stories I have added visual images and background details that come from Biblical research of noted scholars. Not all of them can be completerly verified. For instance it is an ancient tradition but not a scriptural fact, that Ann and Joachim were parents of Mary. The added details and descriptions take nothing away from the Scriptural accounts, but I have found they make the stories more concrete and memorable.

I have selected different characters for the telling, some of whom are fictional, though very likely someone similar was indeed part of the story. As you will see in the second section of this book, I personally like to tell a story from the "first person" point of view. To help you feel comfortable with this approach, I have included marginal notes that give you, as the teller, particular details that the listeners do not have. Some refer you back to Israel's past; some just help make the time or place more vivid.

These stories can take your listeners on journeys from Nazareth and Capernaum to Jerusalem and back. They show Jesus' ministry unfolding at the Jordan River; water turned into wine; fishermen befriended. There are miracles and messages woven into stories told by an apostle, a child, an aunt, a shepherd. The stories here all come from the New Testament, but the Appendix offers three additional original stories that give "background" information. A grandmother tells a story about sheep; Joseph of Arimathea takes us on a trip to see the temple; and a young person tells the story of the first Passover.

I hope you will tell these three early on in your home or school program. It's important to know about sheep to understand why Jesus is not only the Good Shepherd but the Lamb of God. Animal sacrifice is a foreign concept today, but when we tell the story of the visit to the temple and "show" the altar of sacrifice we can explain what Jesus meant by being the Lamb of God who takes away the sins of the world. In addition, so many stories take place at the temple, the children should have a visual image of this historic place of worship. Finally, the first Passover is best told in story so that the connection can be made with the Last Supper and the sacrificial offering that is our liturgy today.

The stories here are stories about Jesus, not the stories Jesus told. There are no parables, no prodigal sons returning or bridesmaids waiting. You will not hear of mustard seeds planted or vineyards producing wild grapes. That is not because Jesus' stories are not important, but because I believe they are the second level of the building and here we are just laying the foundation. Children will be able to understand the stories Jesus told only after they have an understanding of the Jesus who told the stories.

All the interpretations in the world are useless without "the story." We must tell the children that all of this really happened once upon a time and that Jesus still comes through the Spirit to dwell in those who seek him. We must teach them that he is not a faraway God but one who loved us enough to come as a baby, to grow up in obscurity, and to suffer and die so that we might live forever.

I hope you will take these stories and reweave them. Put them in your own voice, own them with your own heart, and tell them with joy to your own unique group of children.

"Did you know him?" Benjamin asked me. "Yes," I whispered, and my eyes teared. "I knew him. He often stayed at a house next to mine, just up the hill from the lake. Mary Salome always told me when he was coming home. I watched for him like a child waits for his father."

"Tell me about him," he pleaded, "tell me everything," and I began…

"Then he told them to go into the whole world and proclaim the good news to all creation."

Mk 16:15

Overview

The stories I have chosen for this book are in sequential order. I believe that is the best way to tell them. One builds on another and there is a sense of expectation of what will happen. The many different characters reveal the Jesus they knew, in the places where he walked. The apostles come to understand who he is, gradually, as they watch and listen to him.

I think it is important that children know the life of Jesus took place in a certain place, at a certain time in history: that he was really here! I also think it is easier to remember things in sequence. When we tell our own story we go from the time we were born in a certain town, and include those events along the way that were milestones.

The stories in this collection give a biographical overview of the life of Jesus that will make it easier for the children to understand the rest of the New Testament teachings. They will give them the "hook" educators speak of, upon which they can attach more abstract material. When children have a sense of the whole story and where the different events happened, they can fit in the small piece of the story they hear on Sunday or read in the weekly lesson. Even if time does not permit you to tell all the stories in sequence, I would suggest that you preface the stories you do tell with a summary of what went before.

Of course, these are not the only stories to tell children. You may want to tell entirely different stories, or parables or stories from the Hebrew Scripture. In this section I would like to share with you my method of preparing stories for telling. You will develop your own style, but it may help you to know what has worked for me.

1. Preparing Stories to Be Told

A. Read More Than One Version; Check the Commentaries.

When storytellers are choosing a fairy tale or a fable to tell, most of them like to read more than one version or translation of the story. One version may include a slight variation, or some detail that is missing in another.

In preparing a Scripture story, I like to read from different Bible translations and from biblical commentaries. Most public libraries have collections of Bibles as well as several commentaries that follow the readings line by line. I also like to see if the story in one gospel is longer or more detailed in another. I find books like *Gospel Parallels: A Comparison of the Synoptic Gospels* (Burton H. Throckmorton, editor, Thomas Nelson, 1992) to be great timesavers in this respect, as comparable readings are on the same page.

B. Research the Setting of the Story

You really have to be able to "see" where the story takes place before you can tell others about it. You may not describe it in much detail in the actual story, but when you know what the scene looks like you will add enough visual detail to let your listeners "see" the setting too. It would be difficult to tell "Little Red Riding Hood" if you had no idea what a forest looked like, or what kind a animal was called a wolf.

When you have a sense of the geography, climate, customs, the Hebrew rituals of Jesus' time, and an image of both Galilee and Jerusalem, you can get inside most of the New Testament stories. Fortunately, hundreds of beautifully illustrated books have been written about the life and times of Jesus. The National Geographic Society and Reader's Digest, for instance, have many books filled with photographs, maps, charts, and facts about Old and New Testament times. These are also available at most public libraries.

Many of the "Life of Christ" books written in the first half of this century are treasures of carefully researched details, word pictures, and stories. The authors of these books have put the three years of Jesus' public life into a sequential order, based on Scripture references to new moons and feast days. That makes it easier to know just when a particular event happened. You can often find these classics at book fairs and church yard sales, as I have. Finally, I look up words, people, and place names in a dictionary/concordance, and check distances on maps.

C. Imagine the Land Where Jesus Walked

As you do your research, you will come to know the villages that are scattered on the hillsides of Galilee, like Nazareth and Cana and the lakeside town that Jesus loved: Capernaum with its soft curve of shoreline, gently rising hills, fleets of wooden boats bobbing on the sapphire sea. You will hear reeds shaking in the wind, birds calling, camel drivers talking with silk merchants at this caravan stop on the way to the Great Middle Sea. You will picture potters and weavers, cloth merchants and blacksmiths at shops on the dusty road; the tax collector at his excise booth; Roman soldiers in red caps.

On the hillsides you will see flocks of sheep, olive trees burdened with fruit, figs ripening under dark leaves; children chasing after dogs and women carrying water from the well. Further on you will see grapes growing in the bright sun near fields of wheat and barley. At the synagogue each Sabbath, you will count day laborers and fishermen sitting with Greek merchants and Jewish scribes.

As you read on, you may take an imaginary four-day journey to Jerusalem, down from the Galilean hills to the wide Jordan valley and onto the waving palms of Jericho.

A wilderness of crags and caves will rise up to the west; resting places for devils and jackals. It will be desert country as you make your way up the steep pass toward the holy city, along the road where the man fell among thieves.

At last you will come to the city on a hill, Jerusalem, David's city, whose twin hills balance on a limestone spur, overlooking a valley of thorn bushes, refuse, and lepers. You will notice a grimy metropolis of a hundred thousand souls; the poor cramped in little cubes of houses that run up the hillside. You will visit international markets in the upper city after passing fish sellers at the fish gate. Sheep and donkeys, dogs and camels will crowd you on the narrow, winding streets.

Then you will be dazzled by the white marble temple on the eastern ridge of the city, as the light flashes off the plates of gold. It is bigger, more magnificent than you might have thought. The temple mount covers thirty-five acres. There are colonnades and towers, a Roman fortress, and at the center, the Sanctuary.

As you stand on Mount Moriah, as Abraham did four thousand years ago, you can see Bethlehem on the hill to the south and Bethany to the east. You have more places to visit: Nazareth, Shechem, Bethsaida Julias, Tiberius, Caesarea Philippi. You attach a mental image to each one, remembering how long it took to get there in a pair of fisherman's sandals…

Naturally, the more you read, the more familiar you will be with the land and the people Jesus knew, and the easier it will be to prepare your stories.

2. Putting the Story Together

After I have selected a story, researched the location, determined who was known to be present, and created a mental picture of where the story takes place—then I stop. I let the story settle in my mind. I reread it, then I live with it for a few days, weeks even, before I decide who will tell this particular story. Sometimes the choice is obvious. At other times it is difficult to think of the right teller for a specific audience, until the subconscious mind works on the story and the character "appears."

A. A Case for the First Person Narrative

Most of the time we hear Bible stories from the narrator's point of view. I think it is both easier and more effective to use the first person to tell a story. You speak with authority when you are an eyewitness; you tell the story from the inside. It is also more natural for an eyewitness to add visual details or pieces of conversation in stories that are spare in description or character development. But even in the story of The Woman at the Well, where the Scripture gives the words of the characters and visual images as well, a first person account still makes the story more alive. Let me show you what I mean. Here is a portion of the story from the Scripture: (John 4:5–10, Jerusalem Bible)

> On the way he came to the Samaritan town called Sychar, near the land that Jacob gave to his son Joseph. Jacob's well was there and Jesus, tired by the journey, sat down by the well. It was about the sixth hour. When a Samaritan woman came to draw water, Jesus said to her, "Give me a drink." The Samaritan woman said to him, "What? You are a Jew and you ask me, a Samaritan for a drink? Jews in fact do not associate with Samaritans."
>
> Jesus replied: "If you only knew what God is offering and who it is that is saying to you: Give me a drink, you would have been the one to ask, and he would have given you living water."
>
> "You have no bucket, sir," she answered, "and the well is deep: how could you get this living water?"

Now let's let the woman tell the story:

> It was noon and very hot when I went to the well that day. Our holy ancestor Jacob gave this well to his son, Joseph, and we thought it was the best water in Samaria. I almost missed him sitting there in the shade. Fetching water was women's work. I moved my veil aside to get a better look, when he spoke to me. He asked me for a drink. He said he had walked a long way and he was thirsty.
>
> I put down my water jug and looked at him, puzzled. I asked him how it was that he a Jew, was asking me, a Samaritan woman, for a drink. I told him I knew Jews did not have anything to do with Samaritans, and anyway men did not speak to women in public!
>
> Then he said something startling. He said that if I knew what God was offering, and who he was that was asking for a drink, then I would have asked him, and he would have given me living water.
>
> I was confused. Living water came from the deep veins of the earth. That was why Jacob had dug this well. Dead water was what we collected in cisterns when it rained. I told him that he had no bucket and the well was very deep, nearly ninety feet. I asked him how in heaven's name he was going to give me living water…

As you can see, the eyewitness is very believable. The woman speaks from personal experience; you can sense her feelings, especially later in the story when she reveals who it was that came to the well that day. The eyewitness can give the listeners supplementary information that is not provided directly in the story. Further, in a first person account you do not have to continually say, "he said," or "she said" for all the characters the way a narrator does. That simplifies the story. Best of all, it is much easier to remember the story when you are the teller. Storytellers don't memorize their stories the way actors memorize scripts. In a first person role you tell about something you remember happening…once upon a time.

B. How to Choose the Right Character

To put a story into the first person you must choose a character who was there, or could have been there. It is quite all right to invent a character who could have been there. While it's easy to see how the Woman at the Well can tell her own story with conviction, you'll find an artisan or fisherman can relate the miracle stories he or she heard in the synagogue; any shepherd can confidently tell about caring for sheep. The boy (or girl) with the leftover lunch easily remembers when his/her lunch fed thousands. It is important to be comfortable with the "voice" of the character, although you will find a woman can tell a man's story as well as a man can tell a biblical woman's story.

You do have to like the character and have a sense of that character's presence in the story. As you read the stories in this book, you may really relate more to one or another of the tellers. You may take a certain character with you into another story. Or you may rewrite the story entirely in another character's voice.

When I look for a character to tell a story, I find some of them seem to come forward and "volunteer" to tell a certain story. They make good tellers. That is why I suggest you let the story settle in your mind for a day or two before you decide who will tell the story.

For this book I was looking for a character who could explain something about the synagogue in Capernaum, to contrast it to the Jerusalem temple. I also needed someone to tell the story of Jesus calling himself the Bread of Life, following the story of the multiplication of the loaves and fish. I didn't even think of Jairus, the president or ruler of the Capernaum synagogue, until I was at the dentist. Then, in one of those moments when the trapped body lets the mind run, I thought of him. I realized how perfect he was because he could also tell of Jesus bringing his daughter back from the dead—a story I had not included. I added the healing of the possessed man because it took place in the synagogue where Jairus presided and he must have seen it. As I thought further, I concluded that Jairus must have gone to Jerusalem for Passover. Surely, he would have heard from Peter, James, and John about the Last Supper, because they were at his house when Jesus raised his daughter from the dead. Jairus could tie the stories of Jesus calling himself the living bread with the institution of the Eucharist. Easy, right? Now all I had to do was to find out more about Jairus, determine the synagogue ruler's duties, and revisit the healing of his daughter and the poor fellow with the demon. But I did have a character who could tie it all together, and make the stories understandable. I had found someone who was an eyewitness.

The more you live in the Scripture, the more you will find yourself drawn into the stories. You will begin to feel John's sense of foreboding at the Last Supper or Mary's fear as she wrapped up her baby's clothes when the angel said to flee to Egypt. You will wonder what some of the unnamed people thought as they saw the man's withered hand made whole, or heard the news that ten outcast lepers were healed. You will find you will want to tell the story from a certain person's point of view.

C. Other Advantages to Selecting a Teller

There are other advantages to choosing a teller: the parent/teacher voice gives way to that of the character. You become someone else during the story—anyone at all! This can be empowering for parents and teachers who are outgoing, as well as for those who might be more reticent. Many actors profess to being introverted and yet they can easily portray an array of characters far different from themselves. The character helps us over our own stage fright.

Getting into a biblical character allows you to tell his or her story with more intensity than you might use in your everyday voice. It also give you the chance to express your own faith in the words you give your character. Becoming a character takes away the self-consciousness that comes from telling the story as a parent or a teacher might see it. In addition, when you use the teller's voice, you automatically keep down the moralizing that makes a story a lesson instead of a gift. There is always that temptation to say: "Did you get it?" A parent or teacher might want to tack on a moral to the story. But stories speak for themselves and settle in differently in each listener. In stories from the Bible we can expect even more of the gentle settling, the soft mist of grace that makes the Word of God grow. We need not add a moral.

3. Rewriting for Telling

A. In Your Own Words

Once you have a character to tell the story, you need to rewrite the story for telling. A told story is different from a story that is read. This is one of the most important concepts to realize as you prepare your own stories. It is a particularly difficult concept for writers who are used to flowing prose and carefully constructed complex sentences. Storytellers have to edit out all unnecessary words, however lovely they may be, and add visual details so the audience can see what is happening. Wordy phrases go and clear images stay. Simple sentences replace complex ones. Think of how you would tell the story of your child's birth, your family tour of the United States, an unexpected letter that arrived, your first job. If you were to write one of these stories for a magazine, you might express yourself differently than if you were just telling the story to a friend. Keep that in mind as you rewrite.

Happily, rewriting the story in your own words also makes the task of learning a story much easier. Your own way of speaking is easier to remember; the same words come back to you as you think of the story, because they are your way of expressing what happened.

Using your own words has another advantage: you can fill in with some believable observation when you can't quite remember the next line! "I could hear the tinkling of the sheep's bells in the distance…" "The mist was rising from the lake as we started out…"

In workshops I have suggested that if you "freeze," forget your place in the story, you can always say, "It was a very hot day." Except for a few weeks in December and January, you will be correct. Many's the new teller who has used that line to buy time, and immediately got back on track with his or her story.

The gospel stories often start or stop abruptly. You may need to add transition phrases to take your character from one part to another or from one story to another.

"We were always up early…"

"I saw him whenever he came to our village…"

"I'll never forget the first time I met his mother, Mary…"

As you write in your own words, you will find comfortable phrases that automatically come to mind to move your story along or to explain a change of place. This makes you more at ease as the teller and adds to the sense of reality you want in your stories: the inside perspective.

B. Telling About the Story is Not Telling the Story

As you write, be sure you are telling the story and not telling about the story. You can use introductory material but that is not the story. See what happens as you read "about" the story of the birth of Moses and then begin the story.

> The Egyptian Pharaoh felt threatened by the way the Israelites were growing in number. He had told the midwives to kill all the boy babies they delivered but they lied and said the Hebrew women were so strong and they delivered their babies before the midwives could arrive. So he decreed every boy baby must be thrown into the river.

Shiphrah was a midwife, here is the part of her story that comes next:

> One day, just after the Pharaoh's decree, I was called to assist at the birth of a Hebrew woman named Jochebed. She was very nervous as her contractions got stronger. She said she hoped the baby was a girl, like her daughter, Miriam. You see, Hebrew girls were permitted to live because they would not be warriors. Hebrew girls were permitted to live because they would make good wives or playthings for the Egyptians.
>
> "Push," I said, "push again," and then I slowly eased the baby into the world. He was a fine looking, healthy boy. I placed him on her tummy and cut the cord that joined them together, but Jochebed began to cry. She trembled as she picked him up. She was afraid for his life, afraid of the river. She hid him the first three months, pretending he was never born.
>
> Then she and her daughter came up with a plan.
>
> They made a little boat for him by covering the bottom of a papyrus basket with black tar. Jochebed kissed her little son and put him in the basket. Then she placed it carefully among the tall silver green reeds near the river bank. The baby was sleeping as the basket gently rocked.
>
> Miriam hid nearby to watch the baby and to pray to our God. She knew the Pharaoh's daughter came down to bathe at this spot on the river. She

> expected she would notice the basket floating on the river in the tall silver-green reeds.

There is a difference as you give the background and then speak in your own words. Always check and see if you are writing the story from the "inside" or the "outside." In this case we could have heard the whole story in the narrator's voice, but isn't the story more alive when Shiphrah begins to speak?(I chose Shiphrah because she is one of the midwives mentioned in the first chapter of Exodus. We don't know that she assisted at the birth of Moses, but she could have, so she makes a good teller.)

C. Story Sequence Makes Sense

It is best to write your story in order from the beginning to the end. When stories are told in real time sequence, they are easier to follow. Readers can deal with flashbacks, but listeners get lost if the story does not follow a sequential order, so it is best to keep flashbacks to a minimum. Your story has to move naturally from the beginning through the middle to the end. There should be movement and a sense of wondering at what will happen—some suspense to keep the listeners interested.

Sometimes, you may need to recall something that happened earlier. Just make sure you're clear in how you do it. "I was just six years old when I first met Jesus," or "I will never forget that day at the Jordan River when I heard the voice of the Father…." These are examples of easy to follow transitions that can take the listeners back to something that happened earlier. They are also conversational and easy to follow.

4. Let's Tell the Story

A. Everyone's A Storyteller

"I will never be able to remember stories the way you do." Storytellers hear this frequently. Yet, everyone tells stories and everyone remembers stories. In workshops I ask participants to tell me their first memory of church, or what they remember of their first communion day, penance, or confirmation.

Often deep memories surface, recollections long forgotten. Usually, the child's voice is heard, even if the teller is sixty. A little girl is asked to lend her first communion dress to an inner city child who will receive the sacrament the following week: she's happy to be asked and remembers every detail of boxing up the dress, the long white stockings, and the veil. She wondered how the girl looked in her dress. A boy spends hours rehearsing to play "the pastor" for kindergarten graduation but he develops the mumps. Sister Mary calls to say he simply has to be there. His mother washes off the greasy, black ointment the doctor prescribed and helps him into the child-sized cassock. His face is swollen beneath the miniature biretta, but he is still able to give out diplomas from the auditorium stage. It's easy to tell, as she speaks, that the woman can still see every detail of the dotted swiss first communion dress; the man admits he treasures the picture his mother always carried of her son, "the priest."

Workshop participants who said they were not able to tell stories in front of a group had no difficulty sharing these kinds of memories. It really was not a fear of storytelling, a fear of speaking in public, but a fear of not knowing the story. In our own stories, we were there and saw it happen. We feel confident in the telling. When we make the Bible stories our own, whether we are telling our children or a classroom full of children, the story will be so real it will seem that we had seen it all happen.

B. Testing Your Learning Style

Once you have chosen a character and have rewritten the story in your own words, you have already learned much of it from the writing. As I mentioned earlier, the words you choose are the words you use when you speak naturally. As you go about learning the story your attention will be on fitting the pieces of the story together, not memorizing individual words.

You will want to read the story through several times: for content, association with the primary characters, sequence, and just to make it your own. Some people will automatically choose to read from their computer screen; they learn better that way. Some need a printed copy, while others like their own handwritten version. Still others would prefer to read the story out loud or to tape the story and listen to it. We all learn just a bit differently, so we will digress here for just a minute for a simplified look at learning styles.

C. A Brief Discussion of Learning Styles

Some of us are predominately visual, others learn better by hearing. Here are some questions to help you see your own learning style.

- Did you learn to read phonetically, sounding out

the letters or did you remember what a word looked like?

- If someone asks you how to spell a word do you spell it one letter at a time or do you see the whole word in your mind?

- Did you say your times tables out loud, hear 6 times 7 is forty-two, or did you see the 6x7=42 in your head?

- Do you give directions by route numbers, street names, how many traffic lights or blocks? Or do you draw a map with the turns, mention the gas station and the flower shop on the corner where you turn?

- Do you like to read a cookbook and check off each carefully measured ingredient, or would you rather see pictures of the preparation of the jambalaya or the cabbage roulades and then follow the image you form?

- Are you comfortable having a conference call on the phone, or would you rather have the conference in person?

- Do you prefer calling an airline/railway/bus for schedules or would you rather see the printed schedule or look it up on the internet?

- Do you remember what your spouse, child, friend asked you to do or do you immediately write it down so later on you can see the message?

- Do you run for the answering machine to see who may have called or do you wait until you can sit with a pen and paper to write down the message?

From these simple questions we would say that the auditory learner prefers the first way and the visual learner the second. Usually, the auditory learner is more "left brain dominant" and the visual learner is more "right brain dominant." Some people are "whole brain" learners using both hemispheres equally well—and of course, there are always variations in between. By our teenage years most of us developed a way to learn from our less dominant side; we found ways to compensate even when we did not know we had a learning style. It does help to know your best way of learning before you try to learn the stories in this book, or prepare your own stories.

For our purposes these are some of the basic differences:

Left Brain Dominant People:	Right Brain Dominant People:
Listen well, learn by hearing	Make pictures from the spoken words
Make good use of the telephone	Prefer face to face conversation
Remember names and words	Remember faces and images
Make an outline before they write	Write first and outline after
Write down notes	Draw images and maps
Go from part to the whole	Go from whole to part
Learn sequentially, one scene then another	See the complete movie
Prefer explanations	Prefer demonstrations

D. A Practice Story

Here is the story of the Transfiguration (Luke 9:28–36) from the New American Bible. It has characters, sequence, and imagery so it will be a good "test" story.

Select a character to tell the story and then ask yourself how you would go about putting the story in order.

> About eight days after this had been said, he took Peter, John and James and went up onto a mountain to pray. While he was praying, his face changed in appearance and his clothes became dazzling white. Suddenly two men were talking with him—Moses and Elijah. They appeared in glory and spoke of his passage which he was about to fulfill in Jerusalem. Peter and those with him had fallen into a deep sleep; but awakening, they saw his glory and likewise saw the two men who were standing with him. When these were leaving, Peter said to Jesus: "Master, how good it is for us to be here. Let us set up three booths, one for you, one for Moses, and one for Elijah." (He did not really know what he was saying.) While he was speaking, a cloud came and overshadowed them and the disciples grew fearful as the others entered it. Then from the cloud came a voice which said, "This is my Son, my Chosen One. Listen to him."
>
> When the voice fell silent, Jesus was there alone. The disciples kept quiet, telling nothing of what they had seen at that time to anyone.

What did you do first? Did you picture each scene? Write down each part? Say the story sequence out loud? Did you get inside Peter, James, or John to feel how your character felt during this mountaintop experience? Could you see it all like a movie? Do you remember the words?

There are no right or wrong answers, but you should know your dominant learning style by how you decided to approach this story. I think we can all profit by a multisensory approach, the "see it, hear it, say it"

method that was actually in vogue in the classrooms of the 1950s. That is how I go about learning a story.

E. The See It, Hear It, Say It Approach

See It: I am one of those people who sees movielike images of scenes, so as I write, I imagine each scene and see my characters in action. In workshops I have participants make what are called "maps" of the story: visual images of the successive scenes. Most people use stick figures and simple drawings in cartoon type boxes that show the story in sequence. For the transfiguration you might show a mountain, then the sunset, then a glorified Jesus, then Moses and Elijah, Peter's three tents, the cloud, and so on.

There are some storytellers who like to "map" out the story in the room where they will tell it. They mentally attach an image to an object in the room from left to right. As they look at that object, the blackboard, flag, window, they see their story image and they know what happens next. I must confess this is not something that works for me, but it is a practice that helps many tellers.

Both visual and auditory learners need to keep the story in sequence. I always put a sequence list at the end of my stories, so as I go over them I can be sure I know what happens next. I consider this part of "see it."

In my version of the Transfiguration, Peter is the storyteller. I would list the sequence this way:

1. James and John and I walked up Mount Tabor with Jesus.

2. The sun set and we slept while he prayed.

3. We awoke to see Jesus in glory, his tunic brighter than the sun.

4. Moses and Elijah appeared and spoke with him about his death.

5. I did not know what to do so I suggested building three booths.

6. A cloud came and covered them.

7. We heard the voice of the Father calling Jesus his beloved Son.

8. We fell to the ground in fear.

9. It was dark again and Jesus was in his red tunic as before.

10. He told us not to tell the others.

11. The next morning we walked down the mountain, wondering.

Hear It: When you take the time to tape record your stories you do three things: you practice telling the story; you find out how it will sound to your listeners, your pace and diction and inflection; and you create a tool for learning and relearning your story. Tapes are also very helpful when you have long stories to learn. When you think you know a part of the story, turn off the tape and say it to yourself. When you draw a blank, turn on the tape again. If you have not told a certain story for a while, the tape is a good way to recall it. My children often grew tired of hearing tapes of Mom playing in the kitchen, but I found them valuable when I was preparing dinner and especially in the car when I was on the way to tell a story.

Say It: It is easy to fool yourself into thinking you know a story. There is a sure test. Tell it! Out loud is best, away from the printed page. Try to tell the whole story at once, even when you know you have forgotten a part. Then check your copy or listen to the tape and try to tell it again. Don't tell yourself about the story—tell the story as you have written it. (I often put myself to sleep by telling myself a story.) Tell the story piece by piece until it is your own. Many of the stories you will use in the classroom or your living room are short. You may be able to record three or four of them at a time and then learn them as needed.

When you are confident about the words of the story (which need not be exactly the same each time you tell the story) again make sure you know all the parts. Make yourself say the "what happens next." Make sure you know that first, we went up the mountain…then the sun set, etc. This "one paragraph following another" is the most important part of learning the story. It is easy to remember very dramatic parts of stories, but sometimes more difficult to remember how you get to those parts. Sequence and chronology keep you on the path. You will find that as you write you will set up word clues to lead you from one scene to another.

5. Some Final Thoughts

Many storytellers use a certain ceremony for opening a story time. Some clap blocks of wood, others play some music, some roll down a screen that indicates story time has begun. Religion teachers often open a large Bible, light a candle, or pray with the class for the inspiration of the Holy Spirit. It is nice to have a consistent way of making the storytelling time special.

Rather than starting right in, I like to introduce the character who is going to tell the story. "Today John, the youngest of the apostles, will tell the story. He and his brother were fishermen, and he is going to tell us what happened one day in Galilee…"

After that I take a few seconds to get into character. Usually, I look down or away, and then when I am ready, I look directly at the audience and begin in the character's voice. I stay in character until the story is completed. I find it best not to interrupt the story for little classroom problems. If I have to stop I use my "own" voice and then return to the character.

You will want to remember to speak slowly and distinctly, breathe from your diaphragm, and look around from child to child as you tell the story. You may notice that some children are so captured by the story, that they lose all notion of anything around them. You will see it in their eyes. And they will probably tell you all they saw, amazed at the pictures that came from your words.

Do not be surprised if there is silence at the end of the story. At first you may think the children did not like the story, but just the opposite is usually true. The silence shows they were indeed taken away from the everyday to the faraway. It takes a few minutes to return to the reality of the classroom, so it is nice to sit quietly for a few minutes when the story ends. (Teachers may then want to talk about the story, noting what children learned through it. Be sure to explain that some details of the story are imaginative and some actually happened in the gospel account.)

I have shared my secrets and my conviction that telling the story is the best way to teach. Now it is up to you to begin. Trust your own abilities: you tell stories throughout the day. Trust the Word of God to nourish and enlighten the children in what can be an empty and dark world. In place of noise and confusion, instant disaster reporting and fear, you can create a quiet place where each child's mind can click and churn with images, faces, words, and journeys that are life changing.

An Angel Comes to Mary

Luke 1:26–38

The angel Gabriel first revealed his name to the prophet Daniel. He foretold the number of years that would pass before the Messiah came. After the long wait, Gabriel came again, this time to Zechariah, while he was preparing the incense in the temple.

Six months later, Gabriel came to Mary in Nazareth. She was fourteen, betrothed but not yet married to Joseph. It is probable, like other young women, she was preparing her linens, spinning and weaving, and preparing her household when the angel came.

Since the second century, legends have abounded about Mary. She is said to have been the daughter of Ann and Joachim, educated at the Jerusalem temple from the time she was three years old. Further, it was said that the high priest called together single men from the house of David in order to have the Lord select a husband for her. Mary was to be given as a bride to the man whose staff bloomed, and upon whose head a dove came to rest. And so, as the legends go, Joseph was that chosen man.

We do know Mary was the fulfillment of the prophecy of Isaiah: "Behold a virgin shall conceive and bear a son, and his name shall be called Emmanuel" (Is 7:14).

Mary was the only eyewitness to the Annunciation, so I have chosen a made-up neighbor named Sarah to tell the story—as Mary told it to her.

An Angel Comes to Mary

Storyteller: Sarah, a neighbor in Nazareth

Nazareth is 1300 feet above sea level

The Mediterranean is 30 miles from Nazareth

Also, onions, lettuce, herbs, beans, cucumbers, walnuts, almonds, apricots, blackberries, pomegranates

It is now called "Mary's well"
Honey was the only sweetener

The time between the betrothal and wedding allowed young girls time to prepare their household

Linen was made from the flax plant

There was a sense of expectation, from those who read the prophets, that the Messiah was about to come

A curtain often was hung at the door leading to the vegetable or kitchen garden

Angel comes from "Angelos" which means messenger

My name is Sarah and I lived just up the lane from Mary in the town of Nazareth. It was a lovely town, on a high plain, surrounded by hills on three sides. From the top of the limestone hills we could see west, all the way to the Mediterranean Sea, or north to the snow covered Mount Hermon. Cool breezes came from the Sea and we had enough rain for our many crops.

We grew olives, figs and dates, melons, wheat, and grapes. We ground barley and wheat into flour to make the bread we baked every other day. We ate fish the men caught and drank spring water the women carried home from the well. When the children were good we baked honey cakes for them.

Most houses were small, just two or three rooms, made of mud bricks and clay. We painted them with a whitewash made from lime and they sparkled as the sun shone on the hillsides.

My neighbor Mary was fourteen when she was engaged to marry Joseph, a carpenter in our town. She was getting everything ready for her house, spinning flax and wool, weaving cloth on an old loom, and caring for her vegetable garden.

Everyone loved Mary. Children from the village followed her when she went to the well. We all thought she was very special, but we did not know how special she was until years later. Mary did not tell us this story until Jesus began to teach. I'll tell it to you just as I heard it.

It seems Mary was in her little house one day weaving some white wool. She began to sing a song asking God to send the Savior—the Messiah that God had promised—the one who would open the gates of heaven. Then a startling thing happened. Suddenly, as she was singing, the curtain at the doorway moved and the small room became filled with a pearl and silver light. In the corner she saw what looked like a very tall man made out of light. He bowed to her and said,

"Hail Mary, you are full of grace, the Lord is with you. You are blessed among women."

It was the Angel Gabriel speaking to her and she was very surprised at his words. She moved back toward the wall but he said, "Do not be afraid, for God is very pleased with you. You will have a son and you will call his name Jesus, for he will save his people from their sins."

Mary was not sure what the Angel meant, so he told her the power of the Holy Spirit would come over her and the child would be—the Son of God.

Mary had just been praying that God would send the Savior but she never imagined she would be chosen to be his mother. She was still trembling when the Angel Gabriel told her that her mother's cousin Elizabeth was also expecting a baby—although she was very old. Gabriel told Mary nothing was impossible for God.

Mary knelt down and crossed her arms in prayer.

"I am the handmaid of the Lord," she whispered, "let it be done unto me according to your word."

The angel Gabriel left without moving the curtain to the kitchen garden.

It was quiet in the little room, some silvery light still reflected off the oil lamp and the shelf of Scripture scrolls. Mary put away her weaving and began to pray. It was hard to believe all the wonderful news. Of all the women in the world, she had been chosen to be the Mother of Jesus. She prayed until evening, repeating again the words she spoke to the angel: Let it be done unto me according to your word.

Then she thought of Elizabeth and she knew she must go and help her. She took her secret with her as she traveled south to the hill country of Judea. Even Joseph did not know the angel had come.

I took care of her garden while she was away but thirty years went by before I learned that Mary's son, Jesus, was the Savior.

Angels usually say, "Do not be afraid"

Mary wondered if the Lord did not accept her pledge as a virgin

There were no books but the Hebrew Scriptures were handwritten on scrolls of parchment

Joseph saw that Mary was pregnant when she returned to Nazareth three months later. He said nothing but decided he must divorce her privately. Then Gabriel came to him in a dream to tell him of the Holy Child

The Visitation

Zechariah and Elizabeth lived in Judea, "in the hill country" is all the Scripture says. A long tradition placed their home in Hebron, south of Bethlehem, in the city where Abraham and Sarah were buried. From the sixth century Ain-Karem, five miles from Jerusalem, has been revered as the place of the birth of John the Baptist.

In either case Mary would have had to make the long eighty-mile journey (a little more to Hebron) to be with her mother's cousin. She would not have made the trip alone. Joseph most likely accompanied her, still unaware that she was carrying Jesus.

Surely, Elizabeth had often seen her cousin's daughter at the temple in Jerusalem, and it is fitting that they should spend the three months together, each awaiting the blessed birth of a holy child. For the Holy Spirit was with each of them and with their sons.

Elizabeth makes a wonderful eyewitness storyteller.

The Visitation

Storyteller: Elizabeth

All day long I had been thinking of Mary. She was my cousin Ann's daughter and she was engaged to be married to a carpenter named Joseph. They lived far away in Nazareth but I couldn't help praying she would visit me. How nice it would be to have her with me as I waited for the baby to come.

I was a bit lonely because my husband couldn't speak. He couldn't say a word! It all happened when the angel Gabriel came to see him in the temple that day. He was preparing the incense in the holy room, when all of a sudden he saw the angel standing next to him.

Gabriel told him not to be afraid because he had brought good news. Angels love to bring good news! Gabriel said that, although I was old, I was still going to have my first baby. He said our son would be very special. He would be filled with the Holy Spirit and when he grew up he would be the one to tell the people the Messiah was coming.

Well, my poor husband, he told the angel it wasn't possible for an old woman and an old man to have a baby. Gabriel said all things were possible with God, but since my husband didn't believe Gabriel, he wouldn't be able to speak until John was born.

As soon as he finished burning the incense he went out of the holy room to bless the people at the temple. No words came out of his mouth.

At first he wrote to me on a waxed tablet. Then he grew tired of it and just stopped writing. I had no other relatives, so you can see why I was praying Mary would come. She was such a kind and generous girl who loved God so. I knew she would be a comfort to me.

God answered my prayer. That very afternoon she came to our house in the hill country!

I rushed to the door and hugged her and when I did the baby I was expecting jumped. He really did! It startled me. Then, at that moment, the Holy Spirit told me Mary was carrying a most wonderful baby. He said Mary was carrying Jesus, the Savior. I

Again it is an old tradition that gives us the names of Mary's parents: Joachim and Ann. Most likely they died before Mary was engaged to Joseph

If you have told the story of the temple the children will know just where this happened

Some sources say that Zechariah was struck dumb as a sign that temple worship was coming to an end, the Old Law was giving way to the New

The people waited twice each day for the blessing that followed the incense burning

Scripture tells us John was filled with the Holy Spirit in his mother's womb. By mentioning the Holy Spirit enlightening Elizabeth in this early story we can begin to prepare the children for the coming of the Holy Spirit at Pentecost

It's nice to remind the children that the first part of the Hail Mary prayer comes from Gabriel's greeting to Mary and the second from Elizabeth's words

Judea was hot and dry, ocher and mauve in contrast to the green hills of Galilee

It's good to use every chance to speak of the value of prayer

Scripture says John grew strong in his soul and lived in the wilderness until the Spirit told him to begin his mission. It is likely he was a teenager when he went off to fast and pray and likely too his parents had gone home to God by then.

stepped back, startled. I bowed and I said: "Blessed are you among women. Blessed is the fruit of your womb."

I stood there for a minute then I asked out loud, "Who am I that the mother of my Lord should come to me?"

Two tears ran down her beautiful, young face and she recited a prayer of thanks to God. You see, she also needed someone to talk to. No one else in the whole world knew that Mary was to be the mother of Jesus.

Mary stayed with me for three months. She helped me spin linen thread and weave fine cloth to make clothes for John. In the late afternoon, when it wasn't so hot, we sat together under the grape arbor and prayed as we worked. Mary said we must pray often because prayer lifts us up to heaven. I know her prayers helped me when it was time for John to be born.

Eight days after his birth, we had a ceremony where we named the baby. The neighbors thought we would call him Zechariah after his old father. I stood up and said his name was to be John. They thought I was mistaken and they gave a waxed tablet to my husband. He wrote in big letters: HIS NAME IS JOHN and immediately Zechariah was able to speak. He prayed a most beautiful prayer.

The neighbors were startled. The news spread all over the hill country. People knew right then that God had blessed our child. But it was a long time before they knew he was the Baptist who would prepare the way for Jesus.

The Birth
of Jesus

Mary and Joseph were living what seemed to be an ordinary life in a little whitewashed house in Nazareth. Joseph had his carpentry shop in a limestone cave behind the house. A baby was expected. Then a messenger came from imperial Rome. There was to be a census, the first census since Rome annexed the Holy Land. Each man was required to return to the land of his forebears to register; Joseph had to go to Bethlehem, David's city.

Only the men had to register but Joseph would not leave Mary just when the baby was due. Mary rode a bony-backed donkey over rutted roads from the hills of Nazareth to the holy city of Jerusalem. They arrived the morning of the fifth day and had just another five hilly miles to travel to Bethlehem. Already the streets were crowded with pilgrims. They were surprised at the numbers. Joseph was nervous, scared there would be no lodgings. When would the baby come? How would he provide?

Mary was peaceful, serene. She knew the Scriptures. The prophet Micah said the Messiah would be born in Bethlehem. It was time and her young heart ached to see the Holy Child she'd so carefully carried for nine months.

Joseph is the storyteller.

The Birth of Jesus

Storyteller: Joseph

"Inns" were hostels for people and animals. They were primitive, walled enclosures with open arcades that faced the courtyard. Animals slept in the courtyards and people in the open arcades

Ornate, oriental lamps now hang over the place where Jesus was born—in the limestone cave. The Church of the Nativity is overhead, just off Manger Square in Bethlehem

Pilgrims and merchants often stayed overnight in Bethlehem when they were on their way to Egypt. I knew that, but it was never crowded like this. Camels and donkeys, dogs and wagons clogged the narrow roads that led into town. People were camped everywhere.

I tied the donkey to a sycamore tree near the town square. Mary sat on a wooden bench and waited while I went from house to house looking for a room to stay in overnight. Little two-room houses fill up fast. "No room, no room, sorry for your trouble, but we've just no room." That was all I heard.

When I went back to tell Mary she was talking to a shepherd boy. He'd just milked his sheep and handed her a tin cup of warm foamy milk. I thanked him for his kindness. "Sir," he said, "the town's full up but there are caves over there, behind the inn. Merchants keep their sheep in them in stormy weather, but there's just an old ox there now. They aren't much but they'd give you some privacy." I thanked him again, but I held out hope that I'd find something better. When he left, Mary whispered it was time for the baby to come. I tried to stay calm as I led the donkey down the path beside the inn. Thank God for the shepherd boy, I thought, thank God for the caves.

I helped Mary down from the donkey and took out my lamp. I hung it up in the damp cave and it startled the old ox. Mary went over and warmed her hands on the quiet beast while I took a tree branch and swept the cave. The straw was wet so I lit a fire in the corner, and then I dried handfuls of hay. I made a bed for Mary with the warm hay and I hung my mantle over the door to keep out the cold.

A thin ray of moonlight crept through a crack in the cave. It shone on Mary as she rested. She said she thought the cave looked like a palace, the cobwebs looked like silver strands and the straw like spun gold.

I tended the fire but the long journey made me tired and I soon fell asleep. The bellow of the ox woke me and then I heard the cry of a tiny child. I began to shake as I looked at Mary illuminated by a heavenly light. "Come and see," she said and I knelt beside her.

She'd already wrapped the baby in the fine linen she'd made. I trembled as I picked him up and stared into his beautiful face. I wrapped the bottom of my tunic around him to warm him and tears poured down my face as I said, "My Lord and my God."

It was sometime later that I heard voices outside and a shepherd boy poked his head into the cave. It was Simon who'd given Mary some milk in the town. His brothers and his father were with him. I told them to come in and their torches lit up the damp cave. When they saw Mary and the baby they fell to their knees and praised God. Then each one offered us gifts: cheese, bread, and a combed sheepskin to keep Jesus warm.

Then Simon told us what had happened in the field. He spoke softly: "We were watching the stars, when I thought I saw a shooting star. As it came closer I saw it was an angel. We all fell to our knees. We were trembling when the angel said, 'Do not be afraid, I bring you great news. Tonight in David's city the Savior has been born. He is Christ the Lord. You will know him by this, you will find him wrapped in swaddling clothes and lying in a manger made for animals.'"

"Then the whole sky was filled with angels. Their brightness dimmed the moonlight and their singing echoed on and on across the distant fields. 'Glory to God in the highest,' they sang 'and peace on earth to all of good will.'"

Simon's father was smiling in wonder. He said we must not stay in this damp cave; he would find a place for us. He came back the following morning with a kind landlady who made room for us in the village. The shepherds visited us often in the year we lived in Bethlehem. They brought Mary wool and milk from the sheep and flowers from the fields.

Animals, angels, and shepherds welcomed him. Kings and emperors didn't even know that he had come. But forever after the story was told: on that holy night in David's city the Savior of the world was born.

Babies were wrapped tightly in strips of linen called swaddling clothes. They believed it kept the baby straight and warm

Try to use a different voice tone here, for the shepherd boy. If you are not comfortable with another voice, rewrite it with Joseph telling the important details

A manger was usually a stone trough used to feed animals

By most accounts the Magi came the following year and we know by the Scripture the Holy Family was living in a house in Bethlehem when they came

The Church of the Nativity in Bethlehem was built over the place venerated since the second century as the place where Jesus was born. It is the oldest Christian church in the world

The Presentation of the Child Jesus

When he was forty days old Joseph and Mary took Jesus to the temple. It was time for the rituals prescribed by the law: the presentation of the first-born child and the purification of his mother. Mosaic law required that every firstborn male be consecrated to the service of the Lord, in memory of the deliverance of the Israelites from bondage in Egypt. In the time of Jesus the tribe of Levi had taken over the actual service in the temple, but parents still had to "redeem" their firstborn son from temple service by an offering. In the time of Jesus the fee was five shekels.

No amount of money could release Jesus from his service to God, but Joseph and Mary carried out the law. It was not necessary to bring the child to the temple but it had become customary so that the child might receive a blessing from the high priest.

Women were considered ritually "unclean" for forty days after the birth of a son and eighty days after the birth of a daughter. They were required to go to the temple and present a year-old lamb, or if they were poor, two turtle doves or two young pigeons. And so Joseph and Mary took Jesus to the temple when he was nearly six weeks old. Mary, who was sinless, was ritually cleansed.

Scripture says Anna the prophetess was there. She is our storyteller.

The Presentation of the Child Jesus

Storyteller: Anna, the prophetess

I was 84 years old when I saw Jesus. I had lived in the temple for over sixty years. All that time our country was under the power of the Roman Empire, and all that time I listened to God—and prayed for the Messiah to come. One day, I was walking through the Court of the Gentiles, when I saw a young couple carrying a baby. I lost count of all the mothers and babies I'd seen in the last sixty years. You see, we had a law that said parents had to pay five shekels to the temple so that their first son did not have to live and work at the temple. It was an old law going back to the time when our people were slaves in Egypt.

I watched the man count out five silver coins and then go over to where they were selling doves. The cages were stacked up high. I could see they were poor when they bought the two doves instead of a lamb. Lambs were expensive.

The man carried the doves and the woman carried the baby up the steps and into the Court of the Women. He gave the officials the coins and the doves. The little birds were taken away to the altar in the court of the priests. The fire was already burning there.

I watched as the couple waited in line for the high priest's blessing. There was something about them, I could feel it in my spirit. Could the child be the Savior, I wondered?

When their turn came the woman handed the baby to the high priest. The baby was awake then and looking around at the strange surroundings. The priest picked him up high in the air, mumbled a small prayer, and handed him back to his mother. He sprinkled her with water and went on to the next mother.

The high priest didn't notice anything but old Simeon did. He hobbled over to them. Oh, Simeon was a holy man. He told me God promised him that he wouldn't die until he had seen the Messiah with his own eyes.

Well, the Holy Spirit must have spoken to him. He asked the mother if he could hold the child. He wrapped his old arms around him as if he were a grandson. He started to laugh and cry at the same time. Then he prayed the most amazing prayer.

"Now I can die, Lord, for I have lived to see the Messiah come,

Anna was from a noble family. She was the daughter of Phanuel of the tribe of Asher. Left a widow after just seven years, she spent the remainder of her days fasting and praying in the temple. She was called a prophetess, one who listened to God and comforted others

According to the prophet Isaiah the Messiah would come as a baby, and not appear full grown. (A child would be born and a son given…)

The Holy Spirit led Simeon to the temple at this particular time

"Now, Lord you can dismiss your servant in peace; you have fulfilled your word. For my eyes have witnessed your saving deed displayed for all people to see: A revealing light to the Gentiles the glory of your people, Israel" (Luke 2:29–32)

Elizabeth was the first to be told by the Holy Spirit that Mary was carrying Jesus. Now Simeon too had been told the identity of Jesus

here he is."

Joseph and Mary—those were the parents—looked at one another. They were surprised that Simeon knew of their holy child. Simeon's face looked sad. He turned to Mary and he told her that a sword would pierce her heart because of this holy child. A look of pain crossed her face, there were tears in her eyes. My heart nearly stopped when I realized the baby truly was Jesus, the Savior.

I went over and introduced myself to Mary and Joseph. I bowed and asked if I too could hold the Child.

How warm and soft he was. He held onto my veil as I prayed a prayer of thanksgiving for having seen him. Then I gave the baby to Joseph and I took Mary in my arms. I told her not to worry, God was with her and he would help her through every trial.

Mary knew that, but I wanted to tell her anyway. She smiled at me and then they left the temple. Simeon and I raised our old arms to heaven. We sang out a song of praise. Just as he promised, God had sent the Savior!

I told everyone I met that I had seen the Holy Child. I told them the Messiah had come to save our people.

A Visit
by the Magi

Introduction   Matthew 2:1-23
_____

The Magi (or "the Three Kings") came to Jerusalem to find the newborn
king of the Jews: They had seen a marvelous star and had followed it.
They went, quite naturally, to see the Judean king, to find out where the
child had been born. They had no idea King Herod was a ruthless, ambi-
tious murderer who had connived with the Romans to be given the title
"King of the Jews." When he heard of the possible birth, he ordered his
scribes to search the Jewish Scriptures and they found the Messiah/King
that the Jews awaited was to be born in Bethlehem.

Herod asked the Magi how long ago the star had appeared and he made
note of it. Then, in a false show of interest he told them to return when
they had found the child, so he, too, might pay his respects. The Magi left
Jerusalem again, guided by the strange moving star which came to rest
over a house in Bethlehem.

Jesus was most likely a year old when the Magi arrived. They probably
lived in a rented house and Joseph undoubtedly worked as a carpenter.

Meanwhile, in order to be rid of the "newborn king," Herod ordered the
slaying of all male babies born in Bethlehem in the last twenty-four
months. An angel came to warn the Magi not to return to Herod, and an
angel came to tell Joseph to flee to Egypt.

This story is told by a fictional character, the homemaker who provided a
house for the Holy Family.

A Visit by the Magi

Storyteller: a Bethlehem homemaker

Groups of houses were joined around a common inside courtyard

Scripture calls them "Wise Men from the East." Legends have named them as Caspar, Melchior, and Balthasar

They brought gold because they knew he was the King, incense because he was really God, and myrrh, a perfume used in embalming, because one day Jesus would die to save all people from their sins

Herod "the Great" had killed his wife and his sons along with hundreds of their followers. At this time he ordered the killing of all boys under two years of age, in order to be sure of killing the "newborn King."

The shepherds came to my house early one morning. They told me the most amazing story about angels filling the sky, and about a holy child who was born in one of the caves. I quickly prepared my extra rooms. I was so happy that they were going to stay in our house.

Mary was very young, beautiful, and a wonderful mother to the baby. Jesus was a happy baby; he hardly ever cried. Joseph made him a wooden cradle that rocked on the hard clay floor. In the afternoon, Mary and I carried it out into the courtyard, so Jesus could sleep under the shade of a fig tree.

When he was six weeks old they took him to the temple in Jerusalem. Months went by peacefully. By summer Jesus started to crawl and then by winter he started to walk. Then one day, strange visitors came from far away.

Some people said they were Persian kings, some said they were astrologers, men who studied the stars. Whoever they were, they were quite a sight in our little village. The three men were dressed in fancy satin robes of white and purple, green and gold. They wore multicolored turbans on their heads. Their camels had ornate saddles made of fine leather trimmed with gold. A dozen servants followed them and the neighbors stared as the cavalcade stopped in front of our house.

They told me they had come a long way by following a star. They said they had come to worship the new King. I brought them out to the courtyard where Mary was sitting with Jesus on her lap. They knelt down, removed their turbans and bowed their heads in prayer. Jesus smiled at them as they gave Mary their gifts of gold, frankincense, and myrrh. She was astonished that these foreigners knew of her Jesus and had brought such wondrous gifts.

Everything seemed so perfect to me. The angels in the shepherds' field, Wise Men following a star—the Savior alive in our world! But everything was not perfect. That night, another angel came and told the Wise Men not to go back to see wicked King Herod, and an angel came to Joseph in a dream. He told

Joseph to take the Child and his mother and flee to Egypt. He said it was not safe for them to stay in Bethlehem.

Joseph took some of the gold the Wise Men had given him and he bought two more donkeys. Mary packed only what could fit on the back of the strongest donkey. She couldn't bring the wooden cradle or the quilts or the mats they slept on. She packed their clothes and the little toy animals Joseph had carved from scraps of wood.

I held Jesus as they fastened their possessions onto the donkeys with some old ropes. Joseph helped Mary onto the brown donkey that had carried her to Bethlehem a year before. I was crying as I handed Jesus to her. The sky was just beginning to turn pink but Bethlehem was still asleep when they made their escape.

They had a long and dangerous journey ahead across the Judean mountains and the yellow sands of the desert. They had to pass the pyramids and the Nile river before they finally reached a safe town, far from anyone they knew. Weeks later some camel drivers told me they made it safely to Egypt and that Joseph found work as a carpenter. It was two or three years before another angel came and told Joseph it was safe to return to Palestine.

They did not come back to live near me in Bethlehem. They went back to Nazareth, up north in Galilee, to the house where the angel Gabriel first came to tell Mary she was to be the mother of Jesus.

I did not see them again until Jesus was teaching in the temple in Jerusalem. But I will never forget the time I used to sing to him as a baby—when no one knew he was the long awaited Savior.

It was a 200-mile trip across the Judean mountains and then the Negev and Sinai deserts. A difficult journey across territory even the Roman soldiers did not like to cross

Many Egyptian towns claim to be the place where the Holy Family lived, but we cannot be sure where they lived

Herod died but his son Archelaus was given rule over Judea. He was just as cruel as his father and so Joseph and Mary returned to their home in Galilee

Jesus Stays
in Jerusalem

They were the silent years: the years the Holy Family spent in Nazareth. Scripture gives only one story from the childhood of Jesus. We can surmise that Mary was his first teacher and that when he was six he began to study the Torah at the town synagogue. We can guess that he played with his cousins, James and John; perhaps they set up camp in some limestone caves or watched over a small flock of sheep. Surely, he learned the carpentry trade from Joseph and helped him in his shop.

The one story given in Scripture is spare in detail but prophetic. It records the first words of Jesus.

The storyteller is Mary Clopas or Mary of Alphaeus (the words mean the same). The third-century bishop and historian Eusebius wrote that Joseph had a brother named Alphaeus. He was married to a woman named Mary. Matthew and Mark list the names of the "brothers" of Jesus as James, Joseph, Simon, and Jude. The word brother and cousin are interchangeable. We read also of Mary Clopas who was at the cross when Jesus died. It is apparent that she was the sister-in-law, rather than the sister of Mary. She then was the mother of the apostles, James and Jude Thaddaeus, as well as Joseph and Simon.

Jesus Stays in Jerusalem

Storyteller: Mary Clopas

As you know we went to Jerusalem each Spring to celebrate Passover. Thousands of people came from all the far-off places where Jews had settled. Hundreds made the journey from our town of Nazareth.

Something happened when we went to Jerusalem the year that Jesus turned 12. At the end of the week, when the festivities were over, all the thousands of people began the return journey to their homes.

The festival lasted eight days

There were great crowds of people, camels, and donkeys leaving by the nine city gates. People pushed and shouted, donkeys brayed. Fathers held up small children so they wouldn't be trampled. It was impossible for all the people from our town to stay together. As usual, we made plans to meet at the first campground, about a day's walk from the city. The men and the older boys usually walked together, while the women and the younger children followed.

Groups traveled together from the different towns. It was safer to travel in groups

We were tired when we stopped to make camp. Mary took out her cooking pots and started to prepare supper, when she looked around for Jesus. She asked Joseph where he was, but Joseph hadn't seen him. She asked my sons, James and John, but they hadn't seen their cousin either. Mary walked all through the camp looking for him. Then she started to tremble; her face turned pale. He was gone.

She left her cooking pots. She and Joseph started right back to Jerusalem. All along the way they stopped other caravans but no one had seen a lost boy. Mary and Joseph went to each of the nine gates to see if there were any messages, but there were none. They looked for him, up and down the crooked streets and narrow alleys of the crowded city. They searched the lower city where poor people lived in one-room flats and they looked for him in the upper city where the wealthy built their mansions.

It was customary to leave important messages at the city gate. Certainly anyone who had found a lost child would have left a message

Many of the poor had been evicted so the rich could build bigger mansions

In the morning, they asked the fish sellers and the cheese makers, the potters and jewelers if they had seen a lost boy. They asked farmers who sold vegetables and merchants who sold spices.

No one had seen a handsome boy of twelve. Mary and Joseph didn't go to the temple because they didn't think a young boy would be at the temple. But finally, after three sorrowful days there was no place left to search. They went up the underground staircase to the Court of the Gentiles. Mary thought she heard his voice coming from one of the porches. She walked closer and saw Jesus standing in the middle of a group of teachers, listening to them and asking them questions.

Mary ran up to him. She was breathing fast.

"Son, why have you done this to us?" she said. "Your father and I have looked for you everywhere. We've been so afraid."

Jesus looked at her and said kindly, "Mother, why did you look for me? Didn't you know that I had to be in my Father's house?"

Mary and Joseph were silent. They did not understand. Mary remembered the words Simeon spoke that day in the temple: "A sword will pierce your heart because of this holy child." It was another sorrow for Mary and she carried it in her heart.

Jesus went back to Nazareth with Mary and Joseph and he did everything they told him. He worked in the carpenter shop with Joseph. They made yokes for oxen, stools and tables, door frames and carriage wheels. Sometimes, he went up to the hills or off to the limestone caves. I'm sure he was praying. But he still liked to camp out with his cousins and to walk in the fields with the sheep.

For the next eighteen years Jesus lived a quiet ordinary life in our little town. Everyone thought he was just the good son of the carpenter, Joseph.

It was common for men to have discussions but rare for a child to be among them. Some sources say Gamaliel, the rabbi, was among those listening to Jesus at this time. He was Paul's teacher

Mary knew well that Jesus came from the Father for a mission. But at twelve he seemed just a child, one who had gotten lost in the city. She was not prepared for his response, but as Scripture says, she kept all these things in her heart

Fleeing to Egypt had been a great sorrow, as well as hearing the words of Simeon in the temple. More sorrow was to come

Jesus is Baptized by John

Introduction

Matthew 3:13–17 Mark 1:9–11
Luke 3:21–22 John 1:29–34

As we learned in the story of the Visitation, Zechariah and Elizabeth were the parents of a holy child named John. At the time of his naming Zechariah spoke in prophecy about his son:

"And you, O child, shall be called the prophet of the most high, for you shall go before the Lord to prepare straight paths for him."

John must have been hidden away when Herod ordered the slaughter of all male infants after the birth of Jesus. We know nothing of his childhood, but the Scripture says he lived in the desert, fasting and praying until it was time to begin his mission. There is no mention of whether the cousins John and Jesus ever met as children or young adults; we have only that scene when John "leaps" in the womb of his mother when Mary comes to visit Elizabeth.

Not a single legitimate prophet had come to the Chosen People in five hundred years, until John appeared at the Jordan ford. Scripture says great crowds came to him from Jerusalem, Judea, and the region around the Jordan: Jews and Gentiles, peasants and Pharisees. To all of them he said, "Repent, the Kingdom of God is at hand."

Another fictional character tells this story so that some of the Old Testament expectations can be included.

Jesus is Baptized by John

Storyteller: Eli, a teenager

Since the days of the exile in Babylon, every town had a synagogue. Cities had many. They were meeting places and houses of prayer where men discussed the Scripture

Booths was the festival celebrating the fall harvest, especially the grape harvest. Families built "tents" in imitation of the vineyard owners' tents or booths—these also came to symbolize the kind of rude shelters the Israelites built in the wilderness. Once again families traveled to Jerusalem for the weeklong feast

The Jordan River brings the melting snows of Mt. Hermon down 200 winding miles to the Dead Sea. In some places it is 14 miles wide while at this ford it is narrow and shallow enough to cross

The Dead Sea is 1300 feet below sea level. There is no outlet and the rapid evaporation of water leaves it full of salt and minerals that prevent any fish from surviving

Scripture says John lived on locusts and wild honey. There were hundreds of kinds of locusts; they tasted like shrimp

My name is Eli, and I lived in Bethany, just outside Jerusalem. My grandfather was the rabbi, the teacher of our small synagogue. He was always talking about the coming of the Messiah, the one who would save us from our sins. He read the words of the holy book and he was sure it was finally time. But he told me someone called a herald would come first to tell the people to get ready. When he came we would know the Lord was coming.

I wanted the Messiah to come in our time so I could meet him! I was glad the feast of Booths was coming and we were going to the Temple in Jerusalem. Maybe the herald would be at the Temple, I thought. Maybe there'd be news.

It was good that we went to the Temple because there was news. They were all talking about it. A man named John was preaching down at the ford, on the lower part of the Jordan river. That's the place where the river is narrow enough to cross. I looked at my brother, Jonas. "The herald," we whispered. We knew just the place. We used to go to the ford in the summer. We'd climb a sycamore tree and watch the caravans of camels, legions of Roman soldiers, and all the strangely dressed people from foreign lands as they crossed the river.

We never went further than this ford, because from there to the Dead Sea it was dangerous. Serpents, jackals, and hyenas lived along the narrow pathway. Bandits hid in the rocks. Even the fish that made it downriver died when they reached the Dead Sea.

My grandfather agreed we could go and see what was happening, as long as we didn't go further than the ford. I think he was as excited as we were.

Each day, the man they called John the Baptist came to the the river. He was very tanned from the desert sun. He had dark eyes, long hair and a black beard that nearly covered his face. He was dressed in a short tunic made out of camel's hair and he had a leather belt around his thin waist.

He told the people they needed to be washed clean, baptized he called it. He said they were to change—stop sinning and live good lives because the Savior was coming. If a person agreed to change his ways, John would dunk him under the water and say a prayer to God. One person told another and soon great crowds gathered along the river bank.

Some people thought John was the Messiah. He said he wasn't even worthy to loosen the sandals of the Messiah. He said he was baptizing with river water, but someone was coming after him. He would baptize the people with the Holy Spirit and with fire.

Jonas and I ran home to tell our grandfather. We were sure John was the herald. "The Messiah's coming, isn't he," I said. "He's coming soon." Grandfather's eyes looked misty as he got up and took a scroll from his book stand. He lit the oil lamp and read from the prophet Malachi.

Malachi was the last of the minor prophets. He wrote of the coming Savior, and of the herald

"Do you think he's the prophet we've been waiting for, Granddad, do you think the Christ is coming?" "There will be a sign," he said, "a voice from heaven will be heard."

We went back to the Jordan ford many times and waited for the sign. Then one day, a man came from up north in Nazareth. He stood in line just like the others. He was tall and strong, with a kindly look on his face. John smiled at him as if they were old friends. They spoke, and I saw John shake his head. "No," he said, the man should baptize him! I wondered what was happening.

Jesus and John were cousins but they probably never met as adults

The man again asked John to baptize him just as he did the others. John dunked him in the cool water of the river. And then the sign came. As the man came up from the water the sky opened and a white dove flew straight down from the heavens. We heard a booming voice say: "This is my beloved Son. In him I am well pleased. Listen to him."

The dove symbolized the Holy Spirit descending on Jesus

We were shaking as we climbed down from the tree. He was the Savior we were waiting for—he was the Christ. We ran home even faster this time. Grandfather was reading when we came in.

"He's here, Granddad, we saw him today," I know I was shouting, I was so excited. Then I told him all that had happened. My grandfather hugged me. There were tears in his eyes as he sang a psalm of praise.

"God made a promise," Grandfather said. "He said he would send the Redeemer." "God never forgets," I said, "God never forgets."

There Was a Wedding in Cana

John 2:1–11

It is likely that Mary was related to the bridegroom in this story. If so, she probably arrived days ahead of the ceremony to help in the preparation of the food. The bridegroom's family was responsible for the wedding feast which usually lasted a week.

The bridegroom and his friends went to the home of the bride and carried her on a litter to the house of the groom. On the way her friends scattered nuts and roasted grain as omens of happiness and fertility. There was great rejoicing, singing, music making, eating, and drinking.

Arriving guests ritually washed their hands and feet at the door of the house, using water from large stone water jars. Such jars would be empty by the time the festivities had gone on for a few days. It was such ritual jars that were filled with water at Jesus' request.

News of this miracle undoubtedly was carried from town to town in Galilee as Jesus began his public life.

There Was a Wedding in Cana

Storyteller: a waiter

We were just plain country people. We didn't have many feasts. Most days we ate the same thing, barley bread dipped in olive oil, fruits or vegetables from our garden, maybe some salted fish. But at weddings we had meats and sauces, plates of steamed vegetables, dates and fancy cakes and plenty of wine.

I remember the time I was a waiter at a wedding in Cana. It was a wonderful celebration. There were tables full of food. The people danced and sang to flutes and harps, tambourines and castanets. Everyone said the bride was beautiful and the groom was brave.

Then, late in the week, I noticed all the wineskins were empty. There was no more wine. I knew the people would speak poorly of the groom's parents for not providing enough wine for the feast. They would talk about it for years. You see, when it was time for your son to marry you were supposed to be sure to have enough food and wine for all the guests.

Mary, the mother of Jesus, was related to the bridegroom. She saw that I was upset and I told her what happened. "Don't worry," she said and she went over and told Jesus. I didn't see what he could do. Certainly he didn't have any wine we could borrow.

Jesus looked at his mother and said that it really wasn't time for him to begin his work. But he smiled at his mother and Mary told me to do whatever he said.

And what did he say? He said to fill the six stone water jars that were on the terrace. We filled the jars with buckets of water from the well. I didn't see what good it would do to have jars of water instead of wine.

Then Jesus told me to take some of the water to the chief steward, the man who was in charge of the wedding. I took a wooden ladle and scooped a cup of the water out of the stone jar. It was dark red. I gave it to the steward to taste. It wasn't water at all but the most wonderful wine he had ever tasted.

"Where did you get this wonderful wine," he asked the bridegroom. "Everyone serves the good wine first and then the poorer wine. You

The poor ate barley bread, the rich wheat bread. Each house had a little kitchen garden. Many had their own olive trees and hand presses to press out the oil

Cana was nine miles from Nazareth

Wedding celebrations usually lasted a week

These were used for purification, but would have been empty by this time. Each jar held about twenty or thirty gallons

The Jews considered wine a holy drink; they usually mixed it with water. Wine also symbolized the law.

have saved the good wine until the end." Then I told them about the water jars that Jesus blessed. They were astonished and so was I.

I was later told that this was the first miracle Jesus performed. I was so happy that I was a waiter the day he changed the water into wine.

Years later I joined his friends for a supper in this same house. This time Peter took some bread and wine and blessed them and offered them to the Father. He prayed that the Holy Spirit would change them into the body and blood of Jesus.

He passed me a piece of the holy bread and he gave me a drink of the holy wine. He told me those who received the body and blood of Jesus would live forever with Jesus in heaven.

There Were So Many Fish

Peter, Andrew, James, and John were fishermen who kept their boats in Capernaum on the northwest shore of the inland lake called the Sea of Galilee. The lake became a place of refuge for Jesus, a place to retreat from the crowds that followed him. Even after their call, the lake remained a place of work for the first four apostles.

Two thirds of Jesus' ministry took place in Galilee; the happy miracle stories come from this northern province. But Jesus' call was gentle and the men's response was gradual. The fishermen and the others only slowly came to know that Jesus was the Son of God.

He taught in the synagogue on Saturdays and the women, the children, and the poor began to believe in him. They brought the sick to him and they knew that God was with him as he healed the blind, the deaf, the lame, lepers, and those afflicted by evil spirits.

The men, including the future apostles, went about their daily work; Peter and Andrew, James and John continued to fish each night. When it was time, Jesus called them. They left their work to follow him.

Simon, whom Jesus renamed Peter, is the storyteller.

There Were So Many Fish

Storyteller: Simon Peter

It takes half a day to walk from Nazareth to Capernaum

Any of the men were allowed to stand up and read from one of the scrolls and then give their opinion of the meaning. Most Jewish men began to study the Scripture when they were six

God often changed people's names when he called them. Abram became Abraham, Sarai became Sarah, Jacob became Israel, etc.

There is a gentle hill at a curve in the lake where crowds could easily hear his voice

The cold streams of melting snow from Mt. Hermon mixed with the warm waters of the lake and attracted great schools of fish

The Sea of Galilee was home to about 43 kinds of fish. Musht is still caught there. It's now called St. Peter's fish

I guess you know that Jesus grew up in Nazareth, a small town in Galilee. When he began his teaching, he decided to live in Capernaum, fifteen miles away. It's a fishing village on the Sea of Galilee, and my brother Andrew and I kept our boats there. The village was always busy because it was on the caravan route, a highway, you might call it, that went from Syria to the Mediterranean Sea.

There were blacksmiths and pottery makers, bakers and butchers' shops next to markets selling fruit and cheese, blankets and copper pots. The streets were often filled with camels carrying baskets of dried fish.

At first Jesus just taught in the synagogue on Saturdays. The people wondered who he was. He seemed to know every word in the holy book. Because he was wise, some people asked him to heal their sick children. He blessed them and immediately they were made well. The word spread that Jesus could heal the sick and more and more people came to see him.

My brother Andrew met Jesus before I did. So did John, one of my partners in the fishing business. They believed he was the Messiah. I just didn't know. I guess I was too busy with my fishing business to really listen to him.

Jesus often walked by the dock when we were mending our nets, or sorting the fish into baskets. One day he told me he was going to call me Peter. I smiled but I kept on working.

Another morning, as I was hanging my nets up to dry, Jesus called to me. There were so many people trying to get near him, Jesus asked if he could teach them from my boat. I rowed out a little way from the shore. The people sat on the grassy hillside and Jesus spoke from the back of my boat.

Afterward, he asked me if we had caught any fish during the night. I told him we had been out all night but there just didn't seem to be any fish.

"Pull out further," he said, "and put down your nets." I thought it was foolish. We didn't fish when the sun was shining on the water. I shrugged my shoulders but I did what he said. In minutes, the net was full of fish. I waved my arms wildly and called to James and John to bring out their boat to help collect all the fish—so my boat wouldn't sink.

I really felt like a fool. I didn't even want to put down the nets and now we had two boatloads of fish. I shook my head and I told Jesus I wasn't really good enough to follow him. He just said again, "Come follow me, I'll make you a fisher of people."

My brother and I left the fishing business that day and followed him.

Although they gave up their fishing business the men still fished for food for the apostles, their families and for the poor

A Storm
on the Lake

Introduction

Matthew 8:23-27
Mark 4:35-41 Luke 8:22-25

Once again, in this story, Jesus is with some of the apostles on Lake Gennesaret which they called the Sea of Galilee. He told them to sail to the eastern shore so he could have some rest after a long day of teaching. The boat was often the best way of escaping the crowds that followed him. Jesus knew of the unpredictable winds and the changeable sea although the apostles didn't think he had much knowledge of either.

He needed to teach the apostles to have faith in him; incidents such as this must have given them hours of conversation on other long nights on the lake.

James of Zebedee, the brother of John, is the storyteller. He and John and their father, Zebedee, were partners in the fishing business with Peter and his brother, Andrew.

A Storm on the Lake

Storyteller: James

One evening, there were so many people crowding around Jesus, he asked us to take him to the other side of the lake. It was just before sunset and the sea was as calm as glass. I knew he wasn't used to boats so I tried to find a comfortable place for him to sit, but he said he was tired and he would sleep in the stern. He took off his blue-gray mantle and rolled it into a little pillow and he went to sleep.

A mantle was the heavier outer garment worn over the thinner tunic

Peter was steering and Andrew was working the sails. Then I saw the storm clouds racing in from the east. We weren't too far from shore, so I told Peter to turn back. All of a sudden a fierce wind swept across the lake and churned the water into huge swells.

Wave after wave hit the boat, lifting it out of the water, smashing it down again. Peter couldn't steer and Andrew had to let down the sails. And through it all Jesus slept. The storm grew worse and the waves crashed over the sides. We bailed out the water as fast as we could but the boat was beginning to sink.

The Sea of Galilee is 700 feet below sea level and is subject to sudden storms that produce roaring waves and a drop of 20 degrees in temperature

In desperation Peter went back to Jesus and woke him up. "Master, don't you care that we're all going to drown?"

Jesus stood up. He held out his arms and said to the wind, "Stop," and to the water, "Be calm." The wind stopped and the sea became as calm as a mountain pond.

"Why were you so afraid?" he said, "don't you have any faith?"

We looked at one another in wonder as we realized even the wind and the rain obeyed him.

Cure of the Paralytic

Matthew 9:1–8
Mark 2:1–12   Luke 5:17–26

Introduction

Here is another story of Jesus' compassion and of the faith of those who believed in him. The men in this story knew Jesus could heal their friend and they believed he would if he could just see the poor man. Hence, they went up the outside staircase to the stick and mud covered roof and made a hole to let down the stretcher.

There had been many other healings but this time Jesus told the man his sins were forgiven. The people knew that only God could forgive sins. The crowds went away amazed saying: "We have never seen anything like this!"

The story seems to have taken place at Peter's house on the lake.

I chose Peter's wife as the storyteller.

Cure of the Paralytic

Storyteller: Peter's wife

Our house was right on the Sea of Galilee. You could see the synagogue from the front door. Jesus often stayed with us there, but when too many people followed after him, he walked up into the hills to pray to his Father.

The people always knew when Jesus was back because the children would see him walking along the road. They would run like little bees flying from house to house telling everyone the Master was in town.

Jesus loved children because of their innocence. The children were loving. They listened carefully to his words. They crowded around him when he walked and they sat up front when he taught.

One day, my husband, Peter, was trying to calm the many people who were looking for Jesus. Peter knew he was away praying in the mountains and might not be back for hours. Then we heard the children shouting, "He's here, the Master is here," and we too rushed out to greet him.

There were hills all around the low-lying lake

Peter told him about all the people that were waiting for him and Jesus said to bring them into the back courtyard. The courtyard was covered by a roof made of reeds and earth to keep off the sun.

Crowds of people came through our house and into the courtyard. Scribes and Pharisees from the Temple in Jerusalem mixed in with the people from the villages. The children squeezed through the doorway and sat in front of Jesus, but still more people waited out on the lake shore. Jesus began to teach the people.

Then I heard an odd noise coming from the roof. I looked up and saw a hole in the roof. Some men were up there taking off the reeds and the earth between the beams. They were making an opening in the roof. As I watched, they began to let down some ropes which were tied to two long poles, attached to a mat. There was a paralyzed man on the mat, a man who could not walk at all. Inch by inch the stretcher came down until the sick man was right in front of Jesus.

Bamboo poles were laid over cyprus beams and then covered with palm leaves, reeds, and thorn branches and sealed with a clay-like mud

It would have been impossible to bring the man into the crowded room, and the friends could not be sure they could get to Jesus before he went off again to the mountains

Jesus looked pleased that the man's friends had gone to all the

The Hebrews at the time believed physical deformity was due to sin

They were accusing him of blasphemy

trouble of opening the roof so that he could heal their friend. He looked at the young man lying on the mat and he said, "Young man, your sins are forgiven."

The temple leaders were sitting behind the children. They did not believe in Jesus. They only came into our house to see if they could catch him doing something wrong. When they heard Jesus say the man's sins were forgiven they turned to one another with angry looks and whispered.

Jesus knew what they were thinking: only God could forgive sins. So Jesus looked right at them and said, "Why are you whispering to one another? Is it easier to say, your sins are forgiven, or to say, get up and walk?"

They didn't answer him so he continued:

"Just to show you that I have the power to forgive sins, I say, young man, get up, take away your stretcher and walk."

The man who was paralyzed sat up slowly, then he stood up and rolled up the mat. The children moved back and made a path so he could walk out of the courtyard. He was grinning as he went out thanking Jesus and giving praise to God. The Temple leaders did not say a word. The people were amazed at the miracle and they too praised God. Everyone realized Jesus could heal souls as well as bodies.

Jesus Feeds Thousands

Introduction

Matthew 14:13–21 Mark 6:32–44
Luke 9:10–17 John 6:1–15

Herod Antipas, the tetrarch or territorial ruler of Galilee, had married his brother Philip's wife, Herodias. John the Baptist spoke out against the union. Herod imprisoned John for his criticism, just as Jesus began his ministry. Ten months went by, and at Herod's birthday dinner, Salome, Herodias' daughter, danced. Herod promised her anything she asked for, and at her mother's direction she asked for the head of John the Baptist on a platter.

News of the beheading reached Jesus at the same time as his apostles were returning from one of their missionary journeys. They were devastated by the news. Only later would Jesus tell the apostles that most of them would also suffer martyrdom.

Jesus continued to reveal the Kingdom of God to the people of Galilee. He multiplied bread and fish and they followed him because of the miracle. But when he told them he was the living bread come down from heaven, many left him.

The storyteller is a boy or girl from Capernaum: a child whose lunch fed thousands. Scripture says it was a boy, but it will not change the story if you tell it as a girl's recollection.

Jesus Feeds Thousands

Storyteller: a boy or girl from Capernaum

Jesus sent the apostles to the surrounding towns to teach, heal the sick, and cast out demons. Some of them were surprised at the way God acted through them. Their joy was short-lived because when they returned to Capernaum they found out that John the Baptist had been beheaded by Herod Antipas

The river here is more like a mountain stream as it empties into the lake

Peter, Andrew and Philip were from Bethsaida

Where Jesus taught was a lonely place, away from any towns or shops. Jesus had gone there to have some time alone with his apostles

I was glad Jesus and his friends lived in our town. I loved to listen to his stories. I knew most of the apostles by name. But after a few months Jesus sent his apostles off to many other towns to tell the people about the Kingdom of God. They were gone for a couple of weeks and everyone was waiting for them to return.

One day I saw Peter and Andrew walking toward home. A big crowd was following them and even more people were following the other apostles. They had told the people from the other towns about Jesus and, of course, they wanted to meet him too.

I ran down the street to Peter's house, where Jesus usually stayed. When I got there, I saw Jesus and the apostles getting into the boats. Some of the townspeople saw them too. They set out on the lake road in the same direction as the boat, north. I ran and told my father and he closed his shop. He stopped to get my mother and the three of us followed the crowd.

My parents didn't want to miss a word of what Jesus had to say. Neither did I. There wasn't much wind on the lake that day. We walked so quickly we arrived at the Jordan River before the boats came near the shore. We crossed over the river to Bethsaida on the eastern shore and we waited. When the apostles walked up from the shore and saw the thousands of people waiting for Jesus, some of them began to grumble.

"We were supposed to have some time alone with you," one said. But Jesus looked at the crowds and said we looked like sheep without a shepherd.

Jesus sat down on a rock and the sick people formed a line. He spoke gently to each one and healed them. Then he spoke to all of us. He told us more about the Kingdom of God and how we were to love one another. Hours went by but no one wanted to leave. I even forgot to eat my lunch.

By evening, the sky turned a brilliant red; it gave a rosy glow to the hillside. Philip suggested that Jesus tell the people to go into the town and buy some food before it was dark.

"You give them something to eat," he told Philip. Philip shook his head and told Jesus even if they had 200 silver coins they could only buy enough bread to give each person a small piece.

"How much bread do you have?" Jesus asked. I was up front, as usual, and I pulled on Andrew's sleeve. I showed him my lunch basket. He told Jesus I had five barley loaves and two fish. Andrew didn't see how that would be any help in feeding thousands and thousands of people. I just watched to see what Jesus would do.

Jesus told the crowds to sit down on the grass in groups of fifty and a hundred. Then he asked for some baskets. I was right next to him as he held up my little barley loaves and then the dried fish. He said a prayer to God the Father, then he broke the bread into tiny pieces and put some in each of the borrowed baskets.

He used a shepherd's knife to cut the fish and he added bits of fish into each basket. Then he told the apostles to pass out the food. They looked at one another frowning, but I took a basket and reached in and found a perfect fish sandwich. Again I reached in and passed out another and another. The apostles watched in surprise and they too picked up baskets and began to pass out sandwiches to the crowd.

Thousands of people ate all they wanted and there was enough left over to fill twelve baskets. There was great excitement in the crowd. People began to shout: "He is the Prophet! He will be our king!"

Jesus didn't come to be a king the way they thought. He went away to the mountains by himself. My parents and I walked back home along the lake shore. The moon was shining on the calm sea. Everyone talked of the miracle: Jesus fed thousands of people with my five barley rolls and two salted fish.

The Synagogue

Introduction   Matthew 9:18–26   Mark 5:21–43*

A thousand years before Jesus was born, King Solomon built a glorious temple in Jerusalem. The Israelites thought it was the most beautiful building in the world. For four hundred years the Jews worshiped there, and then the Babylonians invaded Jerusalem and destroyed the temple.

The Chosen People had to leave Jerusalem and live in far-off places like Egypt, Alexandria, and Babylon. Since they had no temple to go to, they built small houses of prayer they called synagogues. Everywhere the Jews went they built synagogues.

Even after they returned to Jerusalem, and rebuilt the temple, they continued to build local synagogues. Different trade groups had their own, such as the carpenter's synagogue, or the cloth merchant's synagogue. They were also important in the civic community as they were used for meeting houses. No sacrifices took place at the synagogue; the temple was the only place for burnt offerings.

Because Jesus taught in the synagogues in Galilee it is good to know a little more about synagogue services. Jairus, the ruler of the Capernaum synagogue observed other events, as well. He will be our storyteller.

*Also see: Luke 8:40–56 (Raising of the daughter of Jairus)
Mark 1:23–28 and Luke 4:33–37 (Demon cast out in synagogue)
John 6:26–59 (Bread of Life)

The Synagogue

Storyteller: Jairus, leader of the synagogue of Capernaum

I was the ruler or president of the synagogue in Capernaum. It was a lovely small building made of dark basalt rock and decorated with carvings of plants and flowers. Inside there were carved white columns holding up an upstairs gallery. The lower part was divided into three aisles. In the middle was a platform where the reader stood.

We kept scrolls of God's law in a little cupboard behind a curtain at the front of the room. The scrolls were put in leather cases and carefully wrapped in linen. A lamp burned in front of this *tebah* night and day. People came to the synagogue for prayer and for community meetings too. Boys went to school starting at the age of six.

Everyone came to the synagogue on Saturday. Before they arrived I would have someone sprinkle mint on the floor, to purify the air. Then I would take out a certain Bible scroll and choose seven men to read parts of it. Each man would talk about the part he read. Then we would have prayers and blessings. At the end we would sing some Psalms and collect money and food for the poor.

One day Jesus came to our synagogue. He read from a scroll, just like the other men, and then he began to speak. He knew the scroll by heart! He knew the meaning of every word. The people were spellbound. We could tell he was no ordinary rabbi.

Many months later something extraordinary happened to me. My only daughter got very sick. The doctors could not help her. I went to find Jesus. He was walking along the lake road and there were crowds following him. I pushed my way through the crowds and I threw myself on my knees in front of Jesus. I told him my little girl was dying. I begged him to come and heal her. He said he would come, but then other people stopped him on the way. He was still speaking to them when my friend came and told me my daughter was dead. He said I shouldn't bother Jesus anymore. I screamed out in sorrow, but Jesus said not to worry, he said to believe and she would be well. We continued on, walking quickly, but I was still worried.

My house was full of people weeping and wailing. Jesus told

Basalt was a dark volcanic rock that had a glassy appearance

The women and young children most likely sat in the gallery

The scrolls were divided into 153 sections so it took nearly three years to read all of them

Rabbi means teacher

The synoptic gospels record the story of the healing of the woman with a hemorrhage intertwined with the story of Jairus

Bodies decomposed quickly in hot climates so mourners came as soon as a death occurred. Often professional mourners came to cry out over the death

the people to be quiet. He told the flute players to stop playing their sad songs because she wasn't dead. The people laughed at him and he told them to go outside.

Peter, James, and John were with Jesus. My wife took them to our daughter's room. We could all see she wasn't breathing. Jesus took her hand and said, "Little girl, get up." And she did! Life came back into her. She got up from the bed and walked around the room smiling. My wife and I stood there staring at her when Jesus told us to give her something to eat. I brought in some grapes and figs and a jug of water. Tears were rolling down my cheeks as we all praised God for bringing our little girl back from the dead.

I will tell you another story. A few weeks later Jesus fed the thousands of people with five barley loaves and two fish. So there were bigger crowds than ever at the synagogue the following Saturday. Everyone wanted to see Jesus. My wife and daughter were sitting in the upstairs gallery. Jesus saw them and he waved.

Then he looked at the extra large crowd and he told them they only came because he gave them bread to eat. He said we must not work so hard for bread that does not last. He said the real bread that comes down from heaven gives life. The people yelled, "Give us that bread." Then he said the most amazing thing. He said: "I myself am the living bread come down from heaven. If anyone eats of this bread, he will live forever. The bread I give is my flesh for the life of the world. He who eats my flesh and drinks my blood will live forever."

Many of the people left the synagogue shaking their heads and mumbling.

"How can he give us his flesh to eat?" they said. And many of them turned away. They turned away too soon. They never heard about the supper when Jesus changed the bread and wine into his body and blood.

Our family stayed close to the apostles after Jesus returned to heaven. We knew he was the Son of God when he brought our daughter back to life. Then Peter, James, and John told us Jesus would be with us forever in the Holy Eucharist. He really was the Bread of Life.

In the synagogue that day Jesus reminded the people that their ancestors ate manna in the wilderness and yet they died

The people spoke among themselves saying: "Isn't this Jesus the son of Joseph, whose father and mother we know? How could he have come down from heaven?"

The Transfiguration

Matthew 17:1-9

Mark 9:2-10   Luke 9:28-36

Introduction

Scripture does not name the mountain of the Transfiguration. Some sources say it was Mount Hermon, the highest and most northerly mountain in Israel, whose melting snows feed the Jordan. However, since the third century, Mount Tabor, five miles from Nazareth and ten miles from the Mediterranean Sea, has been considered the correct site.

Today a switchback road with thirty hairpin turns leads up to the Franciscan Church of the Transfiguration on the summit. From every direction there are marvelous views of the Holy Land. The mountain itself rises up from the middle of the Plains of Esdraelon where in the time of the Judges Deborah commanded Barak to lead the Israelites to victory over the Canaanites.

Jesus had told the apostles that he was going to suffer, be rejected by the elders, the chief priests, and the scribes. He said he was going to be put to death and then rise again. The apostles did not understand, nor did they really comprehend Jesus as the Son of God. Then came the day of the mountaintop experience.

Peter is the only one of the three who speaks in this story so I have chosen him as the teller.

The Transfiguration

Storyteller: Peter

Mountains were often places of God's revelation. Moses received the Ten Commandments on Mt. Sinai (also called Mt. Horeb). Elijah fled to Horeb four hundred years later. There he heard the still small voice of God and understood God spoke to his people in laws and in prophecy

Moses represented the Law and Elijah the Prophets

A week before the Transfiguration Jesus had said, "You are Peter and upon this rock I will build my church and the gates of hell will not prevail against it"

At the autumn Feast of Tabernacles the Jews built "tents" as reminders of the tents their ancestors lived in as they wandered on their way to the Promised Land. It would have been usual for Peter to suggest building tents, for they were the ordinary dwelling of the nomadic Israelites

John the Baptist heard the Father's voice say this was his beloved Son, the day he baptized Jesus in the Jordan river

It was early spring and the fields were covered with wildflowers when Jesus asked James and his brother John and me to walk up Mount Tabor. It was a funny mountain all by itself. It looked like a loaf of yeast bread. It was about 1,900 feet high, a hard climb for a man like me in his forties. I struggled to keep up with them. As we walked up higher the Sea of Galilee looked like a shiny bit of gray sky.

We were all tired when we reached the top and Jesus told us to rest. We settled on some rocky ground, in the shade of some trees and Jesus went off to pray.

It was dusk. The sun sets quickly in our part of the world and in minutes it was dark. I was half asleep when all of a sudden I was startled by a great light—more brilliant than the sun. We looked over to where Jesus was praying. He was standing with his hands raised and it looked like he was made of white light—brilliant light was shining out of him. Even his red tunic was as white as snow. His face was shining with an incredible light and his eyes were glowing like sapphires.

We fell to our knees, terrified. Then we saw two men come out of the sky to talk with Jesus. I knew in my spirit that one was Moses and the other was Elijah. They talked to Jesus about his coming passion and death.

I thought I should say something. Jesus had just told me I was going to be the leader of the apostles. I called out that it was good for us to be there—I started babbling. I said we could build three tents, one for Jesus, one for Moses, and one for Elijah. I had just finished speaking when a bright cloud came and covered all three of them and we heard the thunderous voice of the Father say:

"This is my beloved Son, in whom I am well pleased. Listen to him."

We fell on the ground and I cried out "Have mercy on me, a sinner." We kept our heads on the ground in terror, and it took a long time before we noticed that all the brightness had gone away and that Jesus was alone again. There was just a slight glow left in his face, a slight shine on his dark red tunic.

He came over to us and called each of us by name and told us not to be afraid. We stood up slowly and I wondered how we would be able to stay near him now that we had seen him in the glory of heaven.

I told Jesus how frightened we had been in that light, and when we heard the voice of the Father. He told us we should not be afraid, that he wanted to show us he was really the Son of God.

The sun began to rise as we started down the mountain. On the way Jesus told us not to tell the other apostles what we had seen, until he had risen from the dead. We didn't talk at all as we made our way down through the carpet of wildflowers.

Many people thought the resurrection of the dead only took place at the end of time

The Cure of the Man Born Blind

John 9:1–41

Most of the healings recorded in the Scripture occurred in Galilee. Even by the time of the triumphant entrance into the city of Jerusalem, most of the hundred thousand residents had not even heard of Jesus. The temple loomed high over the city and hundreds of synagogues were scattered throughout the city districts, but few of the priests or rabbis followed the itinerant preacher from Galilee.

This story took place in Jerusalem about six months before the crucifixion. Jesus had just told the apostles that he was the light of the world when they came upon a blind beggar who was a fixture at the city gate.

The blind man tells his story.

The Cure of the Man Born Blind

Storyteller: The blind man

I was never able to see anything at all. I was blind because parts of my eyes were missing when I was born.

When I grew up, all I could do was beg. I used to sit by the city gate and hope people would feel sorry for me and give me some coins.

Then I heard about a man named Jesus who healed people, deaf people and people who couldn't walk, even lepers. They said he would be in Jerusalem on Saturday, so I went to the gate early and asked everyone I met to tell me when he came.

No work was allowed on Saturday, that was the Sabbath, our day of rest, the day we went to the synagogue or the temple to praise God. I heard people walking in and out the city gates but it was much quieter than on a work day.

"There he is in front of you," someone said and I stood up quickly. A man with a kind voice came up to me and asked me what I wanted. I said that I wanted to see.

After that, I felt something cold and wet, like mud or clay, on my eyelids. The man, Jesus, told me to go and wash off the mud at the pool of Siloam.

At first I felt foolish, my face was dripping with mud. I wondered if someone was trying to trick me but I trusted his kind voice. The pool was in the lower part of the city, but I knew just how to get there. I tapped my stick in front of me as I hurried to the pool.

I put down my stick and collected some water in my hands. I washed my eyes three times. At the third time, I yelled out, "Oh Most High Lord, I can see!" I fell to the ground and shielded my eyes from the bright light. Everything was so beautiful, the buildings, the sky, the people. I got up and walked over to the pool and splashed the cool, clear water. I bent over and saw my own reflection in the water. "So this is what I look like," I said to myself and I began to laugh.

A crowd of people gathered around.

"Isn't he the blind beggar?" one said.

"No, it's someone who looks like him," another one said.

Some lepers lived in the valley of Hinnom, outside the city. They were not permitted to come near people because of their terrible disease

King Hezekiah dug a long tunnel from the Gihon spring to bring extra water into the city in 700 B.C. It was stored in a reservoir called the Pool of Siloam, in case the city was under siege. The pool was on the southern end of Jerusalem, not far from the Hinnom valley where the lepers lived

The Pharisees were known for their strict interpretation of the Mosaic law and the Hebrew traditions

The Pharisees kept a tight reign on the Jewish law. They even had rules on how heavy a woman's earrings could be—lest wearing them on the Sabbath might be considered work. They could not accept the way Jesus cured the sick on the Sabbath. They refused to believe he was the Christ

"It's me, all right," I said, and they asked me how all of a sudden I could see. I told them a man named Jesus put mud on my eyes and told me to wash it off in the pool of Siloam, and when I did I could see. They didn't believe me and they took me to the Pharisees.

These holy men asked me the same question and I told them the same answer. I told them Jesus put mud on my eyes and told me to wash in the pool of Siloam and when I did, I could see.

The Pharisees grumbled. They said Jesus couldn't be a man of God because he worked on the Sabbath, the holy day. I didn't think putting mud on my eyes was work. I knew he had to be a man of God, because I was blind and now I could see.

"Can't God work a miracle on his own day?" I said. But I don't think they wanted to believe that Jesus was the Son of God, the Messiah. They wouldn't believe the miracle. I didn't want to upset them so I said very quietly, "If he could make eyes for me from a little mud, I think God must be with him."

They still wouldn't believe me. They called my mother and father. They asked them if I was really their son. They asked them if I was really born blind. Then they asked them how I could see.

Of course, my parents said I was their son and that I was born blind. They said they did not know how all of a sudden I could see. They said I was thirty years old, and I could speak for myself!

Once again the Pharisees asked me what happened. I said I had already told them the story. I asked them if they wanted to follow Jesus. That made them angry and they told me to go away.

Later that day, Jesus himself came up to me. He told me he was the one who had cured me. His face was as kind as his voice! I bowed down and gave thanks to him. I told him I believed he was the Son of God.

The Raising of Lazarus

Jesus and his apostles often stayed in Bethany at the house of Lazarus and his sisters, Martha and Mary. It was just two miles from Jerusalem, so it was a convenient place to find some rest when they were visiting Jerusalem.

Lazarus was apparently wealthy and a great benefactor to Jesus' mission. He was also well known and well respected among the temple leaders. In the third year of the mission Lazarus was quite ill and yet Jesus did not go to him to heal him. Jesus told Martha and Mary to trust in order to see the glory of God.

His disciples did not understand why he did not heal his good friend, indeed why he did not even arrive in Bethany until Lazarus had been buried for four days. In Jewish belief the soul could stay around the body as long as three days but by the fourth day the person was surely dead. Jesus had raised the son of the widow of Naim and the daughter of Jairus but both were raised on the day they died. This miracle, witnessed by men who had stayed at the house since the burial, could not be discounted by the chief priest and the Pharisees.

The storyteller is Jonas, a fictional cook in the house of Lazarus.

The Raising of Lazarus

Storyteller: Jonas, the cook

Four days had passed since the men rolled a great stone in front of the burial cave. I still couldn't believe the kind man I worked for was dead. His name was Lazarus and he was a close friend of Jesus. In fact, Jesus and his apostles used to stay with us when they visited Jerusalem. Jesus said he always felt at home here in Bethany.

I was the cook and every day since the burial I had prepared fresh vegetables, picked dates and olives, baked bread and honey cakes—but no one wanted to eat. Martha and Mary, the sisters of Lazarus, stayed in the house while leaders from the temple wandered around the yard. I heard them whispering that Jesus healed other people but he didn't even come to see Lazarus when he was dying. I wanted them to go away, and I wanted Jesus to come.

It was later that same day one of the children from the village came running to the house.

"The Master is coming, the Master is coming. I saw him just down the road."

Martha heard them and she washed her face and combed her hair. She went down the path toward the village and I followed her. She was crying when she spoke to Jesus:

"Lord, if you had been here, our brother would not have died," she said. "But even now I know God will give you whatever you ask for."

Jesus held Martha's hands. He told her Lazarus would come back to life.

"I know he will come back to life, he will rise at the end of time," she said.

Then Jesus looked at her with his kind eyes and he said that he was the resurrection and the life and that anyone who believed in him would live forever.

Martha ran back to get her sister, Mary. She walked slowly up to Jesus and said the same thing Martha said:

"Lord, if you had been here, our brother would not have

The Pharisees believed in the resurrection but the Sadducees did not. Caiaphas, the high priest, was a Sadducee

60

died." Mary was crying and Jesus began to cry too.

He asked them where they had buried their brother. They pointed to the limestone caves that were down below the fruit trees. Jesus walked down the pathway that was lined with hedges. All the crowd followed him, watching. Then Jesus told the servants to open the grave.

Martha was upset and told him Lazarus had been buried for four days and that he was surely decayed. Jesus looked right at Martha and he reminded her that if she believed, she would see the glory of God. I had no idea what was going to happen. Jesus again told the servants to open the grave. They ran off to get some picks and levers to pry away the large stone. When they removed the stone Jesus stood in front of the open grave.

There wasn't a sound from the crowd. Jesus raised his hands and thanked his Father for hearing his prayer.

Then he shouted, "Lazarus, come out."

Everyone stared at the open grave. Then very slowly the dead man walked out of the grave with the white burial cloths wrapped around him and a cloth over his face. The people gasped in wonder.

Jesus said to unbind him and give him some clean clothes and some food. I ran to the house to get a tunic and some other servants brought water and cloths to wash the spices off his face and arms.

When we took the cloth off his face he looked around for Jesus. His dark eyes were full of joy as he smiled at the Savior. Jesus smiled back at his friend and Lazarus said, "Thank you, my Lord and God."

It was a most incredible miracle! Jesus had brought Lazarus back from the dead. There was a great celebration that evening. Everyone ate the food I had prepared. But I noticed some of the temple leaders hurrying away to tell the chief priests and the Pharisees what Jesus had done.

Jews were not embalmed and a corpse would surely be decayed after four days and have a rancid smell

Graves were sealed by rolling a large round stone against the opening and then applying a kind of cement seal

They reported to the high priest Caiaphas who said it was better for one man (Jesus) to die than for the whole nation to be destroyed. That day they began to plan his execution

61

Palm Sunday

Introduction

Matthew 21:1-17
Mark 11:1-17 Luke 19:28-46

It was the Sunday before Passover and the city of Jerusalem was crowded with pilgrims. The people from Galilee had set up their white tents as usual, on the top of the Mount of Olives, above the Garden of Gethsemane. Most of them had not seen Jesus since he had raised Lazarus from the dead. The faithful in Jerusalem had not seen him, either. He had avoided going near the city for some time because he knew the Temple leaders wanted to put him to death. Now his hour had come.

When the sun set on the Sabbath the news spread from the city to the countryside: Jesus was at the house of Lazarus in Bethany. He was coming to Jerusalem the next day. Great crowds set out for the little village hoping to see Jesus and the man he had brought back from the dead.

They lined the roadway from Bethany to Jerusalem as the new day dawned. Lazarus tells this story.

Palm Sunday

Storyteller: Lazarus

There were plenty of rumors going around since the day Jesus brought me back from the dead. Some people said the temple leaders wanted to kill Jesus. Some said they wanted to kill me too. Jesus told me he was going into Jerusalem that Sunday morning, so I was ready early. I was surprised when I saw the crowds of people along the roadway, from our property all the way to Jerusalem.

"There he is," some shouted, "and there's Lazarus who was dead." Jesus smiled at the crowds and continued up the eastern slope of Mount Olivet. When we were near Bethphage, Jesus stopped and called over Thomas and Andrew. He told them to go into town where they would find a donkey and a colt tied to a post. He told them to untie them and bring them to him. If anyone asked them why they were taking the animals, they were to say the Master needed them.

Andrew and Thomas did just as Jesus said. They found the beasts and told the owner the Master needed them. Andrew said the owner was so pleased he carefully brushed the mother and her young colt and put a collar of flowers around their necks. Another man took off his green and blue cloak and put in on the beast.

When the people saw Jesus riding on the donkey they took off their cloaks and put them down to make a carpet. Other people broke off branches from the palm trees and waved them like fans. Children threw flowers and waved as Jesus made his way through the narrow streets. The crowds called out:

"Blessed be the King who comes in the name of the Lord" and "Hosanna to the Son of David."

Just before he started down the steep hill from the top of the Mount of Olives, Jesus suddenly stopped and got down from the donkey. He looked across the valley to the temple on the opposite hill. The sun was shining on the white marble and made it gleam like snow. But Jesus looked very sad. He began to cry and he spoke softly, "Jerusalem, Jerusalem, if you had only known the gift of peace that is yours today."

Lazarus was well known and wealthy. Word of his death and resurrection spread through all classes of people

Lazarus' house in Bethany was two miles from Jerusalem, on the eastern slope of the Mount of Olives

The donkey or ass of ancient times was actually a fiery animal, handsome as a horse and used for sacrifice to the pagan gods

The prophet Zechariah said the Messiah would come riding on a colt that had never been ridden. He would be meek yet he would defeat the demon and death. Many of the people would have been familiar with this prophecy

Jerusalem was sacked by the Romans under Titus in 70 A.D. and the temple was completely destroyed

Jesus again sat on the donkey and rode down the steep hillside, across the Kidron brook to the outside wall of the city. Mothers held up their babies and fathers lifted children onto their shoulder so they could see him.

Some Pharisees and scribes pushed through the crowds. They were all dressed up in their fancy robes. They were very angry. They did not like the people calling out Hosanna. They shouted at Jesus:

"Hosannas should be sung only to God!" "Tell the people to be quiet."

Jesus smiled and said, "If I tell them to be quiet, the stones will call out instead."

Jesus walked around the courtyard. He stopped at a table where a money-changer gave a poor blacksmith just a few shekels for all his Roman money. He walked over to where some lambs were tied up. They were bleating and Jesus could see they were sick. No one was allowed to offer sick lambs at the altar, but the men were selling them anyway to some city people who didn't know anything about lambs. Jesus became increasingly upset as he walked quickly all along the portico. He made a whip out of some cords. He turned over the tables of the money-changers and the coins went rolling across the tiled floor. He cut the ropes that held the lambs and opened the cages of the doves. The animals ran toward the gates and the birds flew away.

"My Father's house is a house of prayer," he said, "you have made it a den of thieves."

There was great commotion in the courtyard as the money-changers looked for their coins and the animal sellers tried to find their lambs. Meanwhile, Jesus went over to where many sick people were waiting. They begged Jesus to help them and he healed them of all their diseases. They cried out their thanks to Jesus, just as I did when he brought me back from the dead. We left the temple in the afternoon and walked back to our home in Bethany. It was quiet now along the roadway, but in my mind I could still hear the people shouting: Blessed is the King who comes in the name of the Lord.

The
Last Supper

Introduction

Matthew 26:17-30 Mark 14:22-26
Luke 22:7-39 John 13:1-20

It was time for the last Passover supper. Scripture tells us Jesus told Peter and John to go into Jerusalem where they would see a man carrying a water jar. They were to follow him into a house and ask the householder what room the Teacher and his disciples could use for the Passover. Then they were to prepare the meal as they had done every year: but this year everything changed.

Over and over, as the third year ended, Jesus told his apostles that he was going to suffer and die. They did not want to believe him—even on the eve of his death.

John, the beloved apostle, sat next to Jesus at the supper. He tells this story and the two that follow: The Agony in the Garden and The Trial.

The Last Supper

Storyteller: John, the Apostle

The Last Supper was held in a house located in the upper part of Jerusalem, not far from where Jesus would be brought for the trial

People reclined to eat, leaning on the left arm, eating with the right

God sent ten plagues on the Egyptians; the last was the death of every firstborn man and animal. Jews who followed God's directions were spared

Only servants or mothers washed other people's feet

Dipping bread in sauce and passing it was a sign of friendship

Only unleavened bread was used for Passover, because on the night the Jews were to be ready to flee from Egypt there was no time for bread to rise. No leaven was allowed in Jewish homes at Passover

We had everything ready for the Passover supper, just as the sun set at six o'clock. The upstairs room where we met was a plain, square room with whitewashed walls and a red tiled floor. There was a sideboard on one wall under the shuttered window. Low couches were set up around a low table.

Passover was my favorite holy day when I was a boy. The special dinner was to remind us of when God freed the Jews from slavery in Egypt. It was called Passover because the Angel of Death passed over the houses of all the people who had marked their doorpost with the blood of the lamb.

Peter was just lighting the oil lamp over the table when the Lord arrived. He was wearing a white tunic and a dark red mantle. He began the Seder as usual with the Passover prayers. He passed the first and second cups of wine, and then he stopped. I didn't know what he was going to do. He got up and took off his red mantle and tied a towel around his waist.

He took a pitcher of water and a basin and walked over to Peter and began to wash his feet. Peter didn't want Jesus to wash his feet, but Jesus insisted. He said he was showing us how we were to serve one another. One by one he washed our feet and dried them with a towel.

We continued eating the lamb and the bitter herbs with the red sauce when Jesus spoke again. He said one of us was going to betray him. We were shocked. Not one of us? I was sitting next to Jesus so Peter signaled me to ask him who it was. Jesus said he would give a piece of bread dipped in the sauce to the betrayer. He handed the bread to Judas.

The others didn't hear what Jesus said, and when Judas got up and left the table they thought he was going on an errand for Jesus. Then Jesus told us very gently that it was time for him to give us the gift of love that he promised. He took a new loaf of our unleavened bread and held it up as he prayed to the Father. Then he broke the bread and passed it to us. "Take and eat," he said, "this is my body which will be given for you."

He poured a new cup of wine and offered it to the Father and he passed it to us. "Take this and drink," he said. "This is the cup of my blood, of the new covenant. It will be shed for you and for many for the remission of sins. Do this in memory of me, for I am going away."

I remembered that day in the synagogue in Capernaum when he'd said, "Unless you eat my flesh and drink my blood you will not have life in you," and I began to understand. I bowed my head as I took a piece of the blessed bread and drank from the cup of blessed wine. I tried not to cry.

After this, Jesus told us he was giving us a new commandment, that we were to love one another just as he loved us. I knew then how much he really loved us. He had created a sacrament so he would always be with us in the holy bread and wine.

When he told us again he was leaving us, Peter was very upset. He said he would lay down his life for Jesus. Jesus looked at Peter and he told him that before the rooster crowed at dawn, Peter would three times deny he even knew Jesus. Peter shook his head, "No, Lord," he said, "not me."

When the supper was over Jesus said we were going for a walk. Often in the evening, we walked to one of the gardens outside the city walls. The upper room was located on the top of Mount Zion. We took the long series of winding steps down into the valley in the middle of the city, and then the steep stone steps that led to the city gate. We passed by the pool where the blind man had been cured. The streets were deserted as we walked along the valley of Josaphat beside the Kidron brook.

The moon was full and lit up the valley and the hills. I looked back and saw the moonlight on the temple, the place Jesus called the House of his Father. At the supper he told us in his Father's house there were many dwellings places. I knew he meant in heaven, not the marble temple. He said he was going to prepare a place for each of us in his heavenly kingdom. He said he would come back and take us to heaven when we had finished the work God called us to do.

I wanted him to stay with us just like he was right then. I walked up next to him and he put his hand on my shoulder. It was a warm night but I felt a chill as we crossed the brook.

He most likely used a pottery cup with two handles

Many of the people at the synagogue did not understand. They said the saying was too harsh and they stopped following him that day

Zion is one of the two hills on which the city was built

The Agony
in the Garden

Matthew 26:36–46 Mark 14:32–42
Luke 22:39–46 John 18:1–14

The apostles often went to the Garden of Gethsemane on warm evenings when they were visiting Jerusalem. Gethsemane means olive press. There was an olive press in the garden where the ripe fruit was crushed for its treasure of oil. The grove was on the western hill of the Mount of Olives and it faced Jerusalem. The eleven still did not understand that Jesus was to suffer and die. He had told John that Judas was going to betray him but the others thought Judas had left the supper table to go on an errand.

Just four days before, Jesus had ridden on a donkey over the same bridge they were crossing. The crowds had shouted, "Hosanna in the highest, blessed is he who comes in the name of the Lord." They welcomed him as if he were a king, but this evening they would come after him as if he were a criminal.

John the apostle continues the story.

The Agony in the Garden

Storyteller: John, the Apostle

It took about twenty minutes to walk from the upper room, in the upper city, to the Garden of Olives. It was springtime and the olives were already growing on the old gnarled trees. The moon was overhead and it lit up the silver-green leaves and the tiny olives. I was going to sit down and rest under one old tree when Jesus told me to get Peter and my brother, James. He left the eight other apostles and told the three of us to follow him a bit further up the hill.

I knew this wouldn't be like the time he took the three of us to Mount Tabor. This time Jesus looked so incredibly sad. I didn't know why he looked so sad. We just followed him up the hill. Then he told me his soul was full of sorrow. He said he could die of sorrow. He asked us to stay awake, to watch and pray for him.

Jesus walked up a little further and knelt against a rock. It was getting cold. Peter gathered some sticks to make a fire. The next thing I knew Jesus was calling us. He asked us why we were sleeping when he'd asked us to stay awake and pray. Peter told him we were sorry. He made a bigger fire.

Jesus went away again and prayed. I heard him call out: "Father, if it is possible, let this cup pass from me." A minute went by, then he said, "But not my will, but Your will be done." Later on, I realized he must have been thinking of all he was going to suffer, but I didn't know it that night.

When he called us again, he was trembling. His face was red and his beard was streaked. It looked like he had been sweating blood. He told me an angel had come to strengthen him while we slept.

The third time he woke us, he told us to get up. He said he was going to be betrayed. I could hear some noise in the distance. I saw men coming toward us carrying torches and others with swords and clubs in their hands—as if they were going after some criminal. Then I saw Judas was leading them. Judas. I wondered what could have happened to him. I was sure the Devil had taken hold of him.

Olive trees are among the longest growing of fruit bearing trees—some live a thousand years

Judas had made a deal with the temple leaders to turn Jesus over to them for thirty pieces of silver

He walked up to Jesus and kissed his cheek. Jesus asked him if he was going to betray him with a friend's kiss. Judas didn't answer but the temple guards closed in. They took hold of Jesus. Peter was furious. He took out his sword and struck one of the servants. He cut off his ear. Jesus told him to put away his sword and he touched the man's ear and healed it.

Jesus looked at all of us. He said he could ask the Father to send twelve legions of angels, thousands of angels…but then mankind would not be saved. Heaven would not be opened. Jesus told us he was going to fulfill the mission his Father had given him. He was going to suffer and die—and then rise again.

The guards tied Jesus' hands and put a rope around his neck and led him back toward the upper part of Jerusalem, to the house of the high priest.

Peter and I followed the crowd from a distance while the rest of the apostles ran off. All at once, I knew why Jesus told us they would strike the shepherd and the sheep would scatter. He was the shepherd and we were the sheep.

He was the Good Shepherd who would lay down his life for his sheep. As Peter and I walked slowly along the dark streets of Jerusalem, we realized he was really going to die.

The houses of Annas and his son-in-law, Caiaphas, were located on Mt. Zion in the northwest part of Jerusalem, near to where they had celebrated the Last Supper

The Trial

Matthew 26:47-75 and 27:1-34
Mark 14:43-72 and 15:1-20
Luke 22:47-71 and 23:1
John 18:15-40 and 19:1-16

Introduction

Seventy-one men made up the senate or council of justice called the Sanhedrin. All of Jewish blood they were priests, scribes (doctors of the law), and elders. Although this council once had political power, it could only rule in matters of religious law under Roman occupation.

Caiaphas, the high priest, had already decided it was better to kill Jesus than to risk having his power grow among the Jews. He and his father-in-law Annas were Sadducees, members of the aristocratic, priestly party. They controlled the temple ceremonies and the temple treasury and the Romans kept them in their advantageous position. Any uprising by this man Jesus had to be stopped or the Sadducees might lose their economic and social advantage as temple priests.

Pilate, a weak man, did not want to be part of the killing of someone innocent. He would have freed Jesus but the crowds questioned his loyalty to Rome. In the end, Pilate gave in to the crowds and to his own fears. He ordered the crucifixion of Jesus.

This is a complicated story with many scenes. If you break it up into parts, it will be easier to learn. Young children will need a much simpler version, but I thought it best to write this story for the tellers. The children will hear parts of the trial on Palm Sunday and Good Friday. They will follow the Passion narrative better after you tell them your version of this story.

The Trial

Storyteller: John the Apostle

Annas still held considerable power and it may have been as a courtesy they took Jesus to him first

Only 23 of the 71 Sanhedrin members were needed for a binding vote

It was unlawful to hold a trial at night so an "official" vote could only be taken after sunrise

There was no wind at all that night. The olive trees were motionless. The light from the soldiers' torches gave a reddish glow to the garden as they pulled Jesus along by a rope, as if he were a stray lamb. I heard the echo of their boots on the wooden bridge as they crossed the brook and started back to the city.

The other apostles had run off, but Peter and I stayed, hidden in the darkness. We didn't speak a word. Then we followed the sad procession, staying far enough back so they couldn't see us. Jesus struggled up through the city gate and up the stone steps to the upper city. It's hard to walk when your hands are tied together. The soldiers and the temple leaders took Jesus to Annas, the former high priest, and then to Caiaphas, the present high priest, to put him on trial. Their palaces were next to one another, joined by a courtyard. They were just up the street from where we had the supper.

It's funny, I thought, as we crept along the dark streets, the temple leaders didn't care that Jesus was really the Messiah—he wasn't the kind of Messiah they wanted. They wanted a warrior King, someone who would kill the Romans and take over the world. They did not want the holy Son of God.

Peter and I took the back streets to the palace. I knew one of the servant girls, and she opened the gate and let us into the courtyard. There were seats set in a half circle for the members of the Sanhedrin. One by one they arrived from their homes in the wealthy part of the city.

Jesus stood in front of Caiaphas with his hands still tied and the trial began. They paid two men to testify against Jesus but the two liars couldn't even tell a story that made sense. Caiaphas was getting angry, he needed witnesses. He had to find some way to convince the council to call for Jesus' death. Finally, he yelled at Jesus and asked him if he really was the Son of God.

"I am," Jesus said, "And one day you will see me seated next to my Father when I come in glory."

The high priest screamed and ripped his tunic as if he was

horrified. He looked around the courtyard at the council.

"We don't need any witnesses, he has told us himself. He must die! He called himself the Son of God. What do you say?" From the half circle of chairs voices cried out: "He deserves death."

"Tell us who hit you, if you're a prophet!" they yelled. The soldiers in the courtyard put a blindfold on Jesus and hit him. Peter couldn't stand watching any more. He went over to warm his hands where the servants had lit a charcoal fire. One of the servant girls noticed him and said he was a follower of Jesus. He denied it. A little later, another one said he must be a friend of Jesus because he spoke like someone from Galilee. Peter told her she was wrong. Then the brother of the man whose ear Peter had cut off recognized him. Peter was scared and he yelled out that he didn't even know Jesus.

Just then, they led Jesus across the courtyard to a small cell. It was three o'clock in the morning and a rooster started to crow. Peter knew that Jesus had heard him. Tears poured down Peter's face as he ran from the courtyard. It was just as Jesus said to Peter at the Supper, "Before the rooster crows twice, you will three times deny that you know me."

All over the city the word spread that Jesus had been arrested. When the sun rose the council voted. They said Jesus must die for calling himself the Son of God. Caiaphas ordered the soldiers to take Jesus to the Roman governor because the council didn't have authority to put anyone to death.

Pontius Pilate was staying at Antonia's palace, next to the temple. Crowds lined the streets and watched from their roofs. All along the way the temple leaders tried to get the people on their side. They lied. They said Jesus wanted to destroy the temple and make them slaves to Rome.

Pilate's official residence was in Caesarea on the coast but he was in Jerusalem in case there was trouble during Passover

Pilate looked at Jesus who was already bloody from being beaten. His hands were still tied in front of him. "Are you a king?" he asked. Jesus spoke softly telling him his kingdom was not of this world. Pilate could see Jesus was not a troublemaker. He told the leaders he was not guilty of any crime and

About 100,000 people lived in the overcrowded city of Jerusalem. At Passover many more thousands came from Palestine and the lands beyond

Pilate's wife Claudia sent him a message telling him not to have anything to do with the holy man, Jesus. She said she had been warned in a dream

Crucifixion was a brutal death that the Romans used for political criminals

should be released, but the crowd was in a rage. Pilate sent for more soldiers. It's easy to get people frightened by telling lies. The temple leaders told the people Rome was going to punish the Jews if they let Jesus live. They said we'd lose everything and the temple would be destroyed. One yelled out "crucify him" and another followed. Pilate told them to be silent. He said he didn't find Jesus guilty and neither did Herod.

Then he had an idea. He remembered it was a custom to release a prisoner at Passover. He suggested he release Jesus, since the only other prisoner was a murderer named Barabbas. The crowd yelled back that they wanted Barabbas released. Pilate asked them what he should do with Jesus and they shouted, "Crucify him."

"Crucify your king?" Pilate asked, but the crowd said: "We have no king but Caesar."

Pilate sent Jesus off to be whipped. The soldiers nearly killed him with their whips. They had no mercy as they struck him again and again with their long leather whips. When they finished, Jesus fell to the ground in a pool of his own blood. The soldiers weren't finished. They made a crown out of a hawthorn branch and put it on his head. They put a dirty purple cloth on him and stuck a reed in his hand. Then they bowed down. They laughed and called him king.

Still it was not enough for the crowds. They began to shout at Pilate, that if he did not carry out the sentence of death, he was no friend of Caesar. Pilate didn't want the crowds turning on him. He didn't want any bad reports going to the Emperor. He was afraid of losing his job. He ordered the crucifixion of Jesus. Then he had a bowl of water brought out. He washed his hands and said he was innocent of the blood of Jesus.

The foolish crowd said Jesus' blood was to be upon them and upon their children. I left then and went back to the upper room to tell Mary, his mother. I didn't know how I would tell her they were going to crucify her son.

The Crucifixion of Jesus

The Scripture tells us Mary, the mother of Jesus, Mary Magdalene, Mary Clopas, the mother of the apostles James and Jude and Salome, the mother of James and John were present during the crucifixion along with John, the youngest apostle.

The women either remained in the upper room when the apostles went to the garden after the Last Supper, or they were waiting at the house of Lazarus in Bethany. In either case, John must have gone to tell them the terrible news.

Crucifixion was a slow and tortured death reserved for criminals and runaway slaves. The Romans placed the crosses facing away from Jerusalem, at the top of a small hill at the crossroads so all could see the dying and be warned. From here one road led toward Bethlehem where Jesus was born, one went north to Samaria where Jesus met the woman at the well, one led back to the city of Jerusalem and the western road led to Joppa and the wide Mediterranean Sea—to the ends of the earth where his story would be told.

Salome, the wife of Zebedee and the mother of James and John, tells this story.

The Crucifixion of Jesus

Storyteller: Salome of Zebedee, mother of James and John

Nard was made from the essence of the soft brown moss that grew in the hollows of rocks. It took 200 pounds to make a liter of perfume

Judas had objected that the money spent on the perfumed oil could have been used for the poor. Jesus said the poor would always be with them but he was going to die

Simon came from Cyrene

The Hebrews called the hill Golgotha, and the Latins called it Calvary

Each "criminal" had his crime written out above his head. Pilate had the sign prepared for Jesus. It read "Jesus of Nazareth, King of the Jews." The temple leaders were furious but Pilate said, "What I have written, I have written"

When my son John came into the room we all knew something terrible had happened. Mary, Jesus' holy mother, stood silently against the wall.

"They are going to hang him on a cross," he said.

I screamed, but Mary did not say a word. She knew her son would one day die to make up for the sins of the world. Mary Magdalene knew it too. When she anointed Jesus with expensive nard just the week before, he told her she was anointing him for his death.

We all put on our dark mantles and followed John to the lower part of the city. A Roman soldier on a black horse rode past us in a cloud of dust and then the trumpets sounded. We saw Jesus struggling down the stone steps behind the other prisoners. His face was bruised and streaked with blood. He could hardly walk. John said the soldiers had whipped Jesus. Still they made him carry the heavy cross.

John and Magdalene held Blessed Mother between them so she wouldn't faint when Jesus passed by. Three times he fell down under the weight of the cross. The Roman officer told a strong looking foreign man to carry the cross the rest of the way. I think he was afraid Jesus would die before he reached the top of the hill.

We followed the sad procession out of the city gate and up a small hill just outside the city. The soldiers threw Jesus on the rough cross and pounded the spikes into his wrists and his feet. Mary covered her ears. They raised up the cross and all I could think of was a dying lamb.

The sky turned a dark blue-black. Darkness spread all over Palestine and the people were afraid of the strange darkness in the middle of the day. Yet, some of them still shouted at him. They asked him why he couldn't save himself if he was the king. Others called out for him to perform a miracle.

Some laughed at him as he suffered. They didn't understand that he was suffering and dying for them. He was suffering and dying so that people could live forever. He looked down from the cross and asked God to forgive the people. He said they didn't know what they were doing.

A little later he called to my son John. He asked him to take care of his mother. He told Mary that John was now her son too. Hours went by. Then Jesus called out in great pain. He said even God had abandoned him.

His mother cried there at the foot of the cross because she could do nothing to comfort him. Drops of his blood fell to the ground, until finally he said that everything was finished. Then he said no more.

At that very moment there was an earthquake. The hill split open and cracks formed in the earth from Jerusalem to the Dead Sea. The people went running in every direction with their hands over their heads. Even some of the Roman soldiers looked up and said surely he was the Son of God.

At the moment Jesus died, the heavy purple veil that hung in front of the Holy of Holies at the temple was mysteriously torn from top to bottom. The temple leaders were astounded and scared.

Soon two of the council members who believed in Jesus came with a ladder to take down his body. My son John helped them take the spikes out of his hands and feet. They took his thin, bruised body down and put it into Mary's lap, as she sat at the foot of the cross. She took the crown of thorns off his head and wiped the blood and dirt from his face with her veil. And she cried as she held him as if he were a baby. "My poor, poor son," she said over and over, "my poor son."

The men put the dead savior on a linen cloth and carried him around the back of the hill to a grave Joseph owned. They put spices on his body and wrapped it in fine linen. They could do no more because the sun was setting and the Sabbath was about to begin. So, they rolled a stone in front of the tomb and we all returned to the upper room in great sorrow.

Nicodemus and Joseph of Arimathea were both members of the Sanhedrin. They believed in Jesus and spoke against his death. Joseph had a tomb just on the other side of the place where Jesus was crucified. He received permission from Pilate to bury Jesus there

The Jewish day began at sunset

The Resurrection

Introduction   Luke 24:36–43   John 20:1–23

The Sabbath began with sunset on Good Friday and ended when the sun set again on Saturday. No work of any kind was allowed, so the women could not have anointed the body of Jesus until after sunset on Saturday. They would not have ventured out to Golgotha at night, however, as it was a dangerous place and outside the city walls.

Mary Clopas, the mother of James and Jude, Salome, the mother of James and John, Mary Magdalene, Martha, and Johanna of Chuza were the women who went to the tomb on Sunday morning. They most likely had remained in the city with Mary, the mother of Jesus, after Jesus was buried.

There is no account of the Blessed Mother going to the tomb, but early tradition taught that Jesus appeared to her immediately after his resurrection, perhaps in the upper room. Matthew's gospel account mentions an earthquake and then the descent of an angel who rolled back the stone that had sealed the tomb. His sudden and overpowering appearance stunned the guards who fell down as if dead.

Mary Magdalene, a faithful believer and the woman Jesus once delivered from seven demons, is the storyteller.

The Resurrection

Storyteller: Mary Magdalene

After the sun set on Saturday, we women prepared the spices to anoint Jesus' body. We crushed them into fine powder and mixed them with myrrh, an expensive perfume. Mary told us the Wise Men had given her myrrh when Jesus was just a baby.

I was awake early on the third day. I told Mary that we would anoint him like a king while we waited for his resurrection. We didn't know when or where it would happen. We didn't know if we would see him again while we were on the earth or if we would only see him at the resurrection at the end of time.

It was still dark as we set out for the tomb. A few men with vegetable carts were coming through the city gate, but the rest of the city was asleep. Salome wondered how we would manage to move the great stone that was rolled across the entrance to the tomb.

While we were on our way to the garden tomb, there was another earthquake. It shook the whole hill. We put down our baskets and waited for aftershocks but there were none. I ran ahead to see if the earthquake had moved the stone. When I got there I saw the large round stone had been rolled away and the two guards were lying on the ground, dazed.

I was frightened as I bent down and looked into the tomb. There was nothing in there. The white linen burial cloths were lying on the stone floor. I ran back to the upper room crying. I told the apostles he was gone, that someone must have taken his body.

Peter and John didn't believe me. They followed me back to the tomb. Peter went in first, and saw it was just as I said. He noticed the extra linen cloth we had put over Jesus' head was folded and left on the bench.

They left the garden but I waited there weeping and wondering. After a while I looked in again and it's a good thing I did. This time I saw two angels sitting on the bench where we'd put Jesus' body. One of them asked me why I was crying. I told him someone had taken the body of the Lord and I didn't know where they had put him.

Even though Jesus had brought Lazarus back from the dead, the disciples did not understand what he meant by his own resurrection

A seal had been put on the stone to secure it in place and guards were stationed so that the disciples would not "steal" the body

The earthquake at the time of Jesus' death had frightened all of Jerusalem

While Magdalene ran off to tell the apostles, the other women arrived at the tomb. They saw two angels sitting inside. One asked them why they were looking for the living among the dead. "He is not here, he is risen as he said," the angel told them. They returned to the supper room to tell the apostles

Scripture says that Jesus cast seven demons out of Mary Magdalene. Some say that refers to a mental illness she had. Others say she lived a promiscuous life. In any case she was redeemed and blessed as the first witness to the Resurrection

Luke gives the wonderful account of Cleopas and his companion who met a "stranger" on their way to Emmaus, a town seven miles from Jerusalem. They realized it was Jesus when he blessed the bread as they ate supper with him

The angel smiled and looked out toward the garden and so I turned and looked too. All the flowers had opened with the morning sun, the trees were covered with blossoms. But it was all a blur to me. There was a man standing there but I could barely see him through my tears. I figured he was the gardener. He asked me why I was crying and I told him the Lord's body was missing. I asked him if he had taken it. I wiped my eyes and looked up and he said, "Mary."

It was the Lord!

"Rabboni, my teacher." I shouted. He was alive! He had really risen from the dead. I started to laugh through my tears. I wanted to stay there with him, but he told me to go and tell the apostles that he had risen from the dead.

I ran off singing. On the way I thought of how I had been as good as dead until Jesus changed my life.

"Oh! he can do anything," I said out loud as I ran, "He is Jesus, the Son of God."

I was still singing when I reached the upper room. The rest of the apostles were there with Peter and John.

"I've seen him! Jesus! He's alive! He told me to tell you." They still did not believe me. They said I was a silly woman.

The other women returned to say they too had seen him. Later on, Cleopas and another man rushed in to say they had seen Jesus in Emmaus. Just as they were telling the apostles all that had happened, the room grew bright and we saw Jesus standing in the middle of the room.

"Peace be with you," he said. The apostles were frightened. Some of them thought they were seeing a ghost.

"Why are you afraid?" he said, "Look at my hands and feet, see where they put the nails."

All the men stood absolutely still, amazed at seeing Jesus alive. He looked from one to another and said,

"Have you anything to eat?"

Peter was still shaking as he turned and picked up the platter with the fish. He gave Jesus a piece of roasted fish and he watched as Jesus ate it.

We sat down together then and listened as Jesus told us once again that everything written about the Messiah had to take place. He had to suffer and die and rise on the third day so that people could change their lives and be forgiven.

He had to die so that people could live forever in heaven. It was the only way.

Jesus Appears to Thomas

John 20:24-29

Except for Peter and John, and of course Judas, there are no accounts of where the rest of the apostles went after Jesus was arrested in the Garden. We do know that when Jesus appeared on Easter evening Judas and Thomas were missing. Judas was dead and Thomas was probably wandering.

Back at the time of Lazarus' death, the word had gone out that anyone who knew of the whereabouts of Jesus was to report to the High Priest. When Jesus decided to go to Bethany anyway, the apostles reminded him how dangerous it was. It was Thomas who spoke up then to say "Let us also go, that we may die with him."

In Aramaic the name Thomas means twin and there are sources that say he had a twin sister. Tradition says Thomas went as an apostle to Mesopotamia and India, where he suffered martyrdom.

Thomas tells this confessional story.

Jesus Appears to Thomas

Storyteller: Thomas

When Jesus was arrested, I went away to hide in the hills near Bethlehem. I was so sad. A few days later I went to the upper room, because I didn't know where else to go. All the others were there. They told me Jesus had risen from the dead. They said they had seen him, in that very room. I didn't believe them. Oh, I knew he brought Lazarus back from the dead, but I didn't think he could bring himself back from the dead. I didn't think he would want to see us again because we had run away.

I said I wouldn't believe he had risen from the dead unless I could put my fingers into the nail holes in his hands and touch the place where the sword pierced his side.

Sunday came again and we met for dinner. We had just passed the plate of fish and the honeycombs when John got up to pass the cheese. He seemed to freeze in place. He stared at something across the room. We all looked over and saw Jesus standing there.

Everybody ran to him except me. I backed into the corner. I hoped he wouldn't see me. But he did. "Thomas, come here," he said. I didn't move. "Here's the one who will not believe unless he sees," he said, but he was smiling.

"Come here," he said again. I walked over to him slowly. He held out his hands and told me to put my finger where the nails had been. I slid my hand forward. Jesus gently took my right hand and put my finger into the hole in each wrist. He opened the top of his tunic and took my hand and pushed it down to where the soldier's sword had gone into his side. I could feel his heart beating. I fell to the floor and cried out: "My Lord and my God." I knew he was really God. I knew he had really risen from the dead. "You believe me because you have seen me," he said softly. "But blessed are those who will believe in me without seeing me."

He went over to the table and sat down to have some fish. Afterward, he put his hand on my head and told me just what he told the others the week before. He said he was giving us the power to forgive people's sins. He said we were also to teach people to forgive one another. I knew he had forgiven me for not believing he had risen from the dead. I thought of how important it would be for all people to know they too could have their sins forgiven.

On Easter evening Jesus said to the ten apostles: "Whose sins you shall forgive they are forgiven, and whose sins you shall retain, they are retained."

Breakfast
on the Beach

The gospels record Jesus appearing to the apostles and the disciples both in Jerusalem and in Galilee during the forty days before he returned to heaven. This story is from the appendix to the gospel of John. It takes place on the Sea of Galilee, at the same place where the crowds once sat and listened to Jesus give his sermon on the Beatitudes.

Peter, Andrew, James, and John still had to fish to earn money. It was their livelihood. This night Thomas, Nathanael, and Simon joined them on the quiet lake. Peter was still grieving because he had denied Jesus on the night of the trial. He worried that Jesus would not forgive him. All of them wondered if they would see Jesus again.

Peter tells this story.

Breakfast on the Beach

Storyteller: Peter

These 2,000-foot high mountains on the eastern shore of the lake are now called the Golan Heights

Fishing was done at night and sometimes torches were used to lure the fish to the surface and into the dragnets

Peter was to be the new Good Shepherd, and he too would lay down his life for the sheep

One hot summer night a few weeks after Jesus rose from the dead, six of us went fishing. The lake was perfectly still, and the moon was just rising over the eastern hills. There was no wind at all, so Andrew and I rowed the boat out toward the middle of the lake. As we rowed, I thought about the night of the terrible storm. We all thought we were going to drown, but Jesus stood up and calmed the sea and the wind. How I wished he were still there in the back of the boat.

We dropped anchor and cast the nets out slowly. I was sure the light of the moon would attract plenty of fish. But later, when we pulled in the net it was empty. Again we cast, pulled it in, empty. We tried another part of the lake. Still we caught nothing. The moon was fading and the eastern sky was turning pink. The night was over and we had no fish. An early morning fog covered the western shore when I heard a man call out, "Have you caught anything?"

I couldn't see the man through the fog but I called back, "No, we've caught nothing."

"Put your nets down on the right side of the boat," he said, and we dropped the net slowly. Immediately it was filled with over a hundred fish.

"It's Jesus," John called out, "the man on the shore, it has to be, look at all these fish!"

I jumped into the water and swam the hundred yards to shore. There was a charcoal fire burning on the beach, and Jesus was there waiting for us. I was so happy I couldn't speak. The others brought the boat into shore and Jesus told them to bring some of the fish. He cooked them on the charcoal fire, then he passed out the fish and the bread he'd brought. I remembered the time he blessed the bread and fish and it multiplied to feed thousands of people. Here he was still feeding us.

After we had eaten, Jesus asked me to walk down the rocky beach with him. His arm was around my shoulder as we walked.

"Do you love me more than the others?" he asked.

I told him I did, and he said I was to feed his lambs. Again he asked me if I loved him and I told him I did and he said I was to look after his sheep. Then a third time he asked me if I loved him. I was a little upset. I told him he knew everything, certainly he knew that I loved him. He said, "Feed my sheep."

We walked back toward the boat. John had put out the fire and collected the extra bread. Andrew had emptied the net full of fish onto the boat. The men were sorting them into baskets to be sold in the market. I didn't want to leave; I knew Jesus wasn't coming with us. He blessed us and we waved to him as James and John rowed the boat toward home.

All the way, I kept thinking about the charcoal fire in the courtyard the night he was arrested. Three times I had told people I didn't know him. This morning he made a charcoal fire there on the beach and he asked me three times if I loved him. He wanted me to know he had forgiven me for denying him.

"Feed my sheep." The words echoed in my ears as we came close to shore. I realized Jesus wanted me to take care of the people like a Good Shepherd takes care of his sheep. I knew he also wanted me to tell them that Jesus forgives sins.

Eel, catfish, lamprey, and other fish were considered "unclean" by the Jews and had to be separated from the "clean" fish that could be sold to the Jews

Jesus Ascends
to Heaven

Introduction   Mark 16:15-19 Luke 24:44-53

In the Acts of the Apostles we read that Jesus appeared many times, to show his followers that he was really alive. Following the Resurrection appearances to Mary Magdalene and the other women, he appeared to two disciples on their way to Emmaus, to Peter, and to the eleven in the upper room. He came the following week when Thomas was present and then apparently the apostles went to Galilee.

Here Jesus made breakfast on the beach, and according to Paul's first letter to the Corinthians, he appeared to about five hundred people in Galilee. It was there he told the eleven all authority had been given to him in heaven and on earth and that they were to go and make disciples of every nation, baptizing them in the name of the Father and of the Son and of the Holy Spirit. He said he would be with his people until the end of time.

They went back to Jerusalem because the Lord told them they were to wait in the city for the coming of the Holy Spirit. Then he gathered them together on the Mount of Olives and he ascended to heaven.

James, the brother of John, tells this story.

Jesus Ascends to Heaven

Storyteller: James, the brother of John

We left the lake in Galilee and went back to Jerusalem about a month after Jesus rose from the dead. Once again, we stayed in the upper room, where we had the last supper.

Jesus told us he was leaving. I didn't want him to go. He told me it was good he was going back to the Father, because then he would send the Holy Spirit to be with us always. He promised the Holy Spirit would help us in our mission and remind us of all he had taught us.

We ate one more meal together. Jesus blessed the bread and wine and we said the Our Father prayer. Then we walked down through the city gate and along the Kidron brook to the garden for the last time. We didn't stop. We walked up to the top of the Mount of Olives, to the place we used to camp.

I stood in the same place I had stood when the procession began that Sunday. I remembered how Jesus looked riding on the donkey with the people waving palms.

The afternoon sun gave the clouds a golden edge. Across the valley the city of Jerusalem looked peaceful, as if nothing had happened there. Yet so much had happened. They'd crucified him as if he were a criminal. He proved to all of them he was the Son of God. He rose from the dead.

There were hundreds of people waiting on the hilltop—the shepherds, the man who had been blind, the healed lepers were there, too.

Jesus thanked all the people for believing in him. He thanked the sheep and the birds for being kinder to him than the temple leaders. He said goodbye to his mother and to each of us. Then Jesus went to the middle of the field and stood on a large rock. He seemed to be edged in gold, just like the clouds. His tunic was as white as snow. His eyes sparkled as he looked at us. He raised his hand to bless us and I could still see the place of the nail.

"Go now and tell my story to all the people on the earth."

He began to glow like the sun as he rose up from the rock. He looked like he did that day when Peter and John and I saw him

The apostles continued to meet in the "upper room" and Mary the mother of Jesus was with them. Scripture says there were also some other women, most likely Magdalene, Martha, Mary of Alphaeus, Salome, and perhaps Johanna and other Roman converts.

James of Zebedee (who tells this story) was the first of the apostles to be put to death. He was beheaded by Herod Agrippa about the year 42—twelve years after the death of Jesus

on Mount Tabor. We fell on our knees. A cloud came down from heaven and took him from our sight. Jesus Christ, the Word of God, was gone in an ocean of brightness.

We just stood there looking at the cloud. We were still staring at the sky when two angels appeared. They asked us why we were looking at the sky. They said that Jesus would come back again at the end of time—and his angels would come with him. As we walked slowly back into the city, I could still see his smiling face, etched in gold. I wondered when he would send the Holy Spirit.

The
Coming of
the Holy Spirit

Introduction Acts 2:1–41

Jesus had told the apostles that he would one day return to the Father, but he assured them they would not be abandoned, left like orphans. He would send the Spirit to dwell in them.

In the beginning of the book of Acts, we read of the Spirit falling on the disciples in the upper room, on Saul at the house of Ananias, on the household of Cornelius, and in Samaria. As they believed, the people were filled with the Holy Spirit. They knew the presence of God within themselves. They prayed in tongues, praising God in a prayer language given by the Spirit.

This is our last story, but of course, it is only the beginning of the church. The Lord promised the Holy Spirit would be with his people until the end of time. It is his Spirit that enables us to tell his story.

Peter, the one Jesus chose to lead the new church, is the storyteller.

The Coming of the Holy Spirit

Storyteller: Peter

It might be good to mention today's Liturgy also includes the Word, the Eucharist, and that Jesus taught the apostles to pray the Our Father

Nicodemus also helped Joseph to bury the body of Jesus

Here we might want to mention grace filling the souls of those who keep God's commandments

Pentecost was celebrated fifty days after Passover

Jesus was gone. We knew we would never see him again until we reached heaven. He had told us to stay in Jerusalem, and so we continued to meet in the Upper Room. There were over a hundred and twenty of us disciples, including Mary, the mother of Jesus. I was so grateful she was with us. I was supposed to be the leader of the apostles. I was scared.

I decided we should read the scrolls like we did in the synagogue, and pray to the Father as Jesus taught us. So each day, we had prayer, then we offered the bread and wine as Jesus did, and we received the Holy Eucharist.

Mary always sat in Jesus' place.

We still kept the doors and windows locked. We were afraid of the temple leaders and of the Roman soldiers. I wondered just how long it would be before Jesus sent the Holy Spirit. It was all we talked about.

My brother Andrew remembered the day the Holy Spirit came down on Jesus at the Jordan River. He remembered John the Baptist saying Jesus would one day baptize us with the Holy Spirit and fire.

Nicodemus spoke up. He said Jesus told him that unless people were born again of water and the Holy Spirit, they would not enter the Kingdom of God. Then I reminded them that Jesus said if we kept his commandments, he would ask the Father to send the Holy Spirit to live in us.

A week after Jesus went back to heaven, pilgrims started coming to Jerusalem from many distant cities. It was time for the feast of Pentecost. At this feast we gave thanks to God for the fruit that grew on the trees in the springtime. We had many feasts to thank God for providing us with food. I didn't think about the feast this time, I just kept thinking about the Holy Spirit.

Sunday came. The doors were locked, as usual, and the shutters over the windows were closed. Suddenly, a strong, driving wind blew through the room. It shook the lantern that hung over the table. A globe of fire appeared in the air and it divided so that a flame came over each of us. I was sure I could hear angels singing.

Immediately, everything became clear. We understood all that Jesus had taught us. We were not afraid of anything. We had been filled with the presence of the Holy Spirit—just as Jesus promised. We began to praise God in different languages, languages we had never learned.

The sound of the wind was so great the people in the neighborhood heard it. A crowd gathered outside the house to find out what was happening. As I told you, there were people who had come to the city from far-off places: Egypt and Media, Crete, Cyrene, and even Rome. Each one heard one of us praising God in his own language. They were dumbfounded.

I opened all the shutters and greeted them. Then I went out and told the people Jesus was sent by God to work miracles and bring healing. I said he was put to death by their own leaders with the help of the Romans. But, I told them, God raised Jesus from the dead because he was truly the promised Messiah!

Many of these Jews would not have heard of Jesus, so Peter's announcement was astonishing

The people were shaken. They asked me what they should do. I told them they must change their lives and be baptized, so their sins would be forgiven and they too would receive the Holy Spirit.

We went throughout the city speaking to anyone who would listen. Crowds gathered. As we prayed over them, they too received the Holy Spirit. Thousands of people became followers of Jesus in just a few weeks. It was a mighty start for the new church that would last until the end of time.

The upper room was in the upper part of the city not far from the temple courts

The apostles often taught at Solomon's portico at the temple. They also healed the sick as Jesus had

I wasn't afraid anymore. I knew Jesus was with us by the power of the Holy Spirit.

Three Additional Stories

A Tour
of the Temple

Introduction

King Solomon built the first temple in Jerusalem, fulfilling the dream of his father, King David. When it was completed, about 968 B.C., God spoke to Solomon and told him that if he was obedient to the Lord's statutes and commands, he himself would dwell in the midst of the Israelites. And so he put the Ark of the Covenant, with the Ten Commandments that God gave to Moses, in the sanctuary, the Holy of Holies, in the innermost court of the temple. The ark symbolized the promise or covenant God had made with the chosen people.

This most glorious of buildings was destroyed by the Babylonians in 587 B.C. and the Israelites were sent into exile for seventy years. The precious ark disappeared and was never found. A smaller, lesser temple was built on the same spot, when some of the Jews returned from their Babylonian captivity. This structure remained unaltered until 19 B.C., when Herod the Great began his grand scheme to make a magnificent new temple. He doubled the size of Mount Moriah where the temple stood. He imported stone and precious metals, employed ten thousand men and trained a thousand priests as masons to build the sanctuary. The outer courts of this temple were still being constructed during the life of Jesus. It was not completed until 64 A.D. It was completely destroyed by the Romans under Titus, in 70 A.D.

Synagogues were houses of prayer, meeting places, schools, and community centers. Scrolls of the law and the prophets were kept in the synagogues. From the time of the exile, when it was impossible to go to the temple, every Jewish town had a synagogue. There were hundreds in Jerusalem in Jesus' day, but there was only one temple.

Mary and Joseph presented Jesus to God at the temple when he was an infant. He remained behind at the temple listening to the rabbis while his parents journeyed back toward Galilee the year he was twelve. Jesus must have been tested by the rabbis to become a son of the law when he was 13, and like all good Israelites he must have journeyed to the holy city every year for Passover.

When he was thirty, he came there again as Messiah and Savior to teach and heal. At the end of his mission he cast out the money-changers and, referring to himself, he said he would destroy the "temple" and rebuild it in three days. Jesus wept over Jerusalem as he sat on a donkey that first Palm Sunday. He said not one stone of the temple would be left upon another.

All over the Diaspora, Jews prayed facing the temple. The Ark of the Covenant was long gone but God's presence was never forgotten. All that remains of the Second Temple today is part of the lower wall which the Jews call the Wailing Wall. The Temple Mount belongs to the Moslems. The Dome of the Rock and the El Aqsa Mosque now stand on Mount Moriah, the place where Abraham brought his son Isaac to be sacrificed, where David built an altar, and where Solomon built his temple.

Once you form an image of the temple in your own mind, you can take your listeners on an unforgettable journey to the temple of Jesus' day. When you tell this story you should move around, use plenty of gestures, and point out the various sites. Add your own sights, sounds, and smells. Perhaps, as has happened to me, the children will grab onto their chairs when you warn them of the long fall from Solomon's Portico.

I chose Joseph of Arimathea, a member of the Sanhedrin and a secret follower of Jesus, to tell this story.

A Tour of the Temple

Storyteller: Joseph of Arimathea

Today we're going on a trip to Jerusalem to see the holy temple. Ready? We'll start right here at the top of Mount Olivet. This hilltop was a favorite campground for the apostles. Jesus and his friends always stayed here when they came to Jerusalem.

If you look over there to the west, you can see the city of Jerusalem. It's a very old city built on two hills. Like all old cities it is surrounded by a great wall for protection. On every side there are arched passageways through the thick walls. Each one has double wooden gates that are locked at night.

That's the temple right in front of you. You can just see the top of the red tiled roofs that surround the Gentiles' court. The tall marble and gold building in the center is the sanctuary and those towers in the far corner are part of Antonia's palace.

We'll walk down from this campsite and through the garden of olive trees. The road is steep, be careful. Do you hear the soft rustling of the leaves? Some of these olive trees are four hundred years old. This garden is the place where Jesus was arrested after the Last Supper.

We'll keep going west and cross the Kidron brook, here on the wooden bridge, and follow the path up the other side of the valley. If we go through the city gate that's right in front of us, the one they call the golden Gate, we will be inside the city and inside the temple walls. This is the gate Jesus went through on Palm Sunday.

We'll take this long staircase up and now we are outside again, in what we call the Court of the Gentiles. It's big enough to hold three football fields, but you can see it is covered with stone pavement instead of grass. It's really more like a meeting place for people from all over the world.

Look around and you can see there the porches all around this courtyard. Those hundreds of tall carved pillars hold up the tile roof which is lined with cedar. It's hot in Jerusalem and the people usually gather under these porches to get out of the sun.

Come over to this side. If you look back you can see where we walked. There's the campground on the top of the hill, and the olive garden further down. There's the Kidron brook and the valley. We call this side Solomon's portico, but be careful. Don't go too close to the edge—it's 400 feet down to the valley.

We had better continue our tour. Look over there. Do you see those little lambs tied up and the pigeons and doves in those cages waiting to be sold for temple sacrifice? The oxen are making a terrible racket. Maybe they know what's coming.

You see, our people were required to buy pigeons, doves, sheep, goats, or oxen and then have them burned in sacrifice. It was the only way our sins could be forgiven. The animals or birds were burned to ashes at a special altar further inside the temple buildings. I'll show it to you when we get there.

We also brought animals to offer in thanksgiving to God. These were not burned up, but cooked and then eaten by the priests and the people who brought them. When Jesus came he changed everything. He stopped the sacrifice of animals. He told us God did not want animal sacrifice. He said he would die to make up for our sins. Then we would be able to confess our sins and if we were sorry, God would forgive us.

I suppose you can see why John the Baptist called Jesus the Lamb of God who takes away the sins of the world.

Do you hear that noise? Some people seem to be arguing. I think it's those men sitting at tables. They're money-changers. Each man was required to give a half shekel to the temple every year. Many people were paid in Roman or Greek money and they had to change it into temple coins. I'm afraid most of the money-changers cheat the people and give them only part of what they should receive.

It's very busy today, and noisy. It's more like a marketplace than a holy place. We'll keep going. As we go up these next steps you can see there's another wall all around another courtyard. There are three doors or gates leading in, we'll go in through this middle one called the Beautiful Gate. Now we're in a smaller outdoor courtyard. This one has rooms at each corner for storing things. This is called the "Court of the Women" but

After Jesus' fast in the desert the Devil took him to the "pinnacle of the Temple" and suggested he throw himself down and have the angels catch him. Solomon's portico was known as the pinnacle of the temple

Often the poor would be sold sick animals that the priests would reject for temple sacrifice

This is a good time to point out the Lamb of God prayer that is said before Communion

At Passover especially the money-changers would charge exorbitant rates to Jews who could only use the temple shekel

The door is called the Gate of Nicanor after the Jew from Alexandria who gave it to the temple. It takes twenty men to open this heavy bronze door. Nothing happens in Jerusalem until that door is opened each morning

Only priests can enter this court

The Shew or "show" Bread is replaced each Sabbath

The archangel Gabriel came to Zechariah while he was preparing incense here

This curtain was torn from top to bottom at the moment Jesus died

A goat was also taken to the desert on the Day of Atonement. The high priest laid hands on him and he carried away the sins of the people. He was called the scapegoat

If you tell this story at the beginning of your class year or your home story time, then the children will have an image to relate to when a story happens at the temple

Jewish men and children are allowed in here too. You can see by that sign anyone who isn't Jewish is not allowed in here.

Let's go up these fifteen curved steps and through this great bronze door. This court is different. See, it's just a long and narrow court we call the "Court of the Israelites." Only Jewish men can go in here. They like to come here to discuss the law of Moses. Behind this white railing and up those three steps is the Court of the Priests. Over there on the left you can see the altar of sacrifice I was telling you about. A fire burns there day and night. It's where the lambs and doves, pigeons and oxen are killed and then burned in sacrifice. Some of the animal's blood is smeared on those horns at the end of the altar. We believe the blood holds the essence of life. Since life belongs to God we put some blood on God's altar.

Now we're coming to the actual temple, that high marble building decorated with plates of gold. Since we are on an imaginary journey, we'll go through this first curtain. This room is divided into two parts. This front part is called "the Holy." There's the table with 12 loaves of bread and the holder with seven candles. Over there is the incense altar. One of the priests lights incense here every morning and every afternoon. Then he goes out and blesses the people. We'll have to go through this heavy embroidered purple curtain to see the back part. This is called the "Holy of Holies." See, it's completely empty, except for that rock where once a year, on the Day of Atonement, the high priest goes in alone and lights incense and prays for forgiveness.

The two stone tablets with the Ten Commandments used to be in here, in a chest carved out of olive wood. The chest was called the Ark of the Covenant. The Ark was taken 500 years before Jesus was born, and was never found. But we Jews believed the invisible God was present in the Holy of Holies. It was the reason we came to the temple for all the feast days.

Then Jesus came. Jesus, the Son of God, died for our sins. When he went back to heaven he sent the Holy Spirit to live in each person who believed in him. There was no more need for temple worship. No more need for offering animals in sacrifice or lighting incense on the Day of Atonement. Jesus told us each person who believed in him became a temple of the Holy Spirit.

Passover
in Jerusalem

Introduction   *Exodus 7:8–29 and 8:1–51*

This story of the first Passover will help the children to see why Jesus and the apostles celebrated the Passover supper. It is always valuable to show the connection between the Hebrew Scriptures and the New Testament. Ideally, we would tell the stories from the Hebrew Scriptures first, and then the connections would be more obvious.

Until we can do that, let's remind children of God's care for the Chosen People, his guidance and direction from the time of Abraham, and his promise that one day he would send the Savior. Show them that the Passover Seder in the upper room became the Eucharistic banquet; the God hidden in the clouds on Mount Sinai became present in the breaking of the bread.

In stories such as this where there are so many specific things to remember, such as the ten plagues, you may want to make a chart. You can refer to the chart as you let the children think about the impact of each plague. There is enough to remember in the Passover story without having to memorize the sequence of the plagues.

I have chosen a young person to tell this story.

Passover in Jerusalem

Storyteller: a young person from Galilee

Groups would travel together for safety and camaraderie. Most people camped outside the city

Famine brought the Chosen People to Egypt and while Jacob's son Joseph was given great power by Pharaoh they prospered. Later, as they grew in number they were made slaves lest they rise up and overtake Egypt. God spoke to Moses from the burning bush. He promised to deliver the people from slavery, with Moses as their leader

Since God told Moses the people must be ready to flee, they could not put yeast in the bread, as there was no time for it to rise

From the 14th to the 21st day of the month they were to eat no leavened bread, nor have any yeast in their houses

Every year the people from our village went to Jerusalem to celebrate Passover. It's in the spring so the fields were covered with wildflowers and the fruit trees were in blossom. Newborn lambs were always playing on the hillsides. We made camp each night and sang songs around the fire. Usually one of the fathers would tell the story of the Passover so the younger kids would understand why we were going to Jerusalem. Maybe you would like to hear this story?

Long ago, our people were made slaves by Pharaoh in the land of Egypt. They prayed to God for freedom and God heard their prayer. God spoke to a man named Moses and told him he would lead our people out of slavery. He would lead them to the promised land—that is our land—Israel. Pharaoh didn't like the idea of losing his slaves. He said the people couldn't leave. So God sent plagues. He turned the water of the Nile river into blood; frogs covered the land; lice and fleas swarmed over the people and animals. Things were so terrible, Pharaoh told Moses to take the people and go. Then he changed his mind! So God sent more trouble.

Swarms of mosquitoes came with clouds of flies. Many of the animals got sick and died. Then, festering sores formed on the Egyptians and on their animals. Again Pharaoh said our people could go—and then he changed his mind. Next God sent hail down to destroy the growing crops; locusts swarmed in and ate everything that was left; then the sun stopped shining and the land was dark. Still Pharaoh would not let the people go.

Then God told Moses he was sending a terrible tenth plague. Moses told our people to do just what God commanded. He said each family should buy a lamb, and on the fourteenth day of the month offer it in sacrifice to God. Then, Moses said they were to put some of the blood of the lamb on the two doorposts and over the doors of their houses. After that, they were to roast the lamb and eat it with sauces and certain herbs and with bread that was made without yeast. Everyone did as Moses told them. During that night the oldest child and the oldest animal in every Egyptian home died. But nothing happened to our people who had put the blood of the lamb around their door. You see, the Angel of Death passed over their houses because they had obeyed God.

Pharaoh was very upset. The Egyptians were calling out in sorrow. Pharaoh sent for Moses and told him to take the people out of Egypt at once. The Hebrew people were overjoyed. Their ancestors had lived in the foreign land of Egypt for four hundred years. Now they were finally going home. And God was going with them. During the day, God showed them where to go by having a cloud lead them. At night, God sent a pillar of fire to light the way. God led them toward the Red Sea, where they made camp at the base of the mountains.

Then Pharaoh changed his mind again! He sent his army after the Hebrews. The sea was in front of them, the mountains on either side of them, and now the Egyptian army was in back of them. They didn't know what to do. The cloud led them closer to the sea, and when they reached the shore, God told Moses to hold out his staff toward the water. All at once a wind came and blew the water into great walls. A path formed through the water and all our people and all the animals walked across the bottom of the dry sea.

A little later, the Egyptian army reached the edge of the sea. They saw the path. They rode their horses and chariots into the dry bottom of the sea. When they were halfway across, God told Moses to hold out his staff again, and the walls of water crashed down. All of the Egyptian army drowned in the bottom of the sea. Meanwhile, all the people of Israel were safe on the other side.

God led our people for the next forty years, until they reached the Promised Land. And every year at the Passover dinner we said the same prayers our people had said for thirteen hundred years. We blessed and praised God for taking our people out of slavery in Egypt.

A Shepherd's Story

Introduction

For thousands of years sheep have grazed the hillsides of the Holy Land. Abraham, Moses, and David were among the many shepherds who cared for their flocks on the same fields where sheep graze today.

The people of Jesus' day easily related to the image of Jesus as Good Shepherd. They often saw a shepherd coming down the hillside carrying a lost or wounded sheep on his shoulders. They knew his long staff was used to rescue a little one who might have fallen off a cliffside, and his club was used to chase away jackals and wolves.

Shepherds were not highly regarded by the religious leaders because pasturing the flocks meant they could not keep all the Jewish laws. Their rough, homespun garments and goathair capes did not look "presentable."

Yet they were the first to welcome the newborn Child. Jesus used them as models of how God cares for his people. This story will help children to understand a little more about shepherds and sheep.

The storyteller is a grandmother.

A Shepherd's Story

Storyteller: a grandmother

Jesus loved children and sheep. I did too. I was surrounded by children and then grandchildren—and sheep.

You have to care for children, watch them and keep them from harm, just the way you have to care for sheep. Sheep need lots of help. They will eat poison plants or gobble up all the sweet herbs if we don't check the fields before they graze. We have to dig up the thistles and nettles that can cut a sheep's soft, black nose.

We lived in dangerous country for sheep. There were mountains with sheer cliffs, caves with wild animals and fast running streams where sheep could drown. The Syrian sheep we raised have no defenses. They can't run fast. They have no claws or sharp teeth. They can't even see very well and have no sense of direction. When we take them to pasture, we make them follow the shepherd in a single line. The children and the dogs follow after them.

Shepherds know each one of their sheep by name. And every sheep knows the sound of his shepherd's voice. Most of the shepherds also have a special call.

In the evening my sons would gather their many different flocks, and put them into one field that was surrounded by a stone wall. The sheep would enter the sheep gate, one by one, and the shepherds would check each one for cuts or sores. They would put oil on any cuts and they'd usually pat each one on the head to welcome him home. One shepherd had to keep guard all night or wolves or jackals might attack the flock.

In the morning, each of my sons would give his special call and his sheep would gather together and follow him out to the pasture to graze. The sheep trusted the shepherd. They knew he would take care of them.

In the Spring, it starts to get very hot where we live, so the shepherds take the sheep up to the mountains where it is cooler. The night before they leave they brush them carefully, tie ribbons around their necks and in the morning they lead them through the town. The villagers line the streets. They wave and

This is the "preparing the table" mentioned in the 23rd Psalm

Still waters are the only places the sheep will drink

The Valley of the Shadow of Death is an actual pass where it is very dangerous for sheep because it is so narrow and full of sheer cliffs

The shepherd uses his rod to throw at predators and his staff to reach down and pick up a fallen lamb

Jesus said whoever did not enter by the sheep gate was a marauder. The 23rd Psalm also speaks of God anointing our head with oil—the overflowing cup refers to the refreshing spring water the shepherd gives the sheep out of an earthenware crock

Jesus was there one day as they were getting ready to leave for the mountains. He told the shepherds they were lucky to be far away for the summer. He said they could hear God in the wind and in the songs of the birds better than in the markets or the cities.

"I am the Good Shepherd," Jesus said, "and I know my sheep and my sheep know me. The people that follow me know that I will care for them, they listen as I speak to their hearts, just the way your sheep listen to you."

My grandchildren were there that day. Jesus told them they must keep wolves away from their hearts the way the shepherds kept wolves away from the sheep.

Little Jonas asked him what he meant.

"You know how wolves act," he said, "they are very clever. They watch the herd from the high hills, then they sneak up through the bushes. When they are close by they stay very still. They look like big gray stones scattered in the pasture. When they think no one is watching, they spring out and attack a sheep who is all alone.

"The devil is like a wolf," Jesus said. "He roams about quietly, and when he thinks no one is watching, he leaps out and tries to make people sin. He whispers selfish thoughts when you are tired or sad and he stirs up trouble the way wolves do."

Then he said, "Some people act like wolves too. They try to make you do things that are wrong. But you must always remember that God and your Angel are always with you to help you when the devil comes, or when people around you act like wolves."

Jesus told us again that he was the Good Shepherd.

He said a good shepherd would even give his own life to protect his sheep. Jesus said he would give his life for us. After that he waved goodbye to the parade of sheep and the shepherds in their goathair capes, and he went on to the next village.

Jonas asked me what Jesus meant when he said he would give his life for us. I couldn't answer him just then. It was only later, when they put Jesus on the cross in Jerusalem, that I knew what he meant.

"Jesus died to save us from our sins," I told my grandson. "Jesus gave his life, so that we, his sheep, could live forever."

Jesus always stresses obedience—his obedience to the Father and our obedience to the commandments—especially his new commandments to love God above all things and our neighbor as ourselves

Here is another chance to remind the children of their guardian angel

Of Related Interest...

Acting Out the Gospels
40 Five-Minute Plays for Education and Worship
Mary Kathleen Glavich, S.N.D.

These ready-made playlets (for grades 4 to 8) are easy-to-duplicate, based directly on Scripture, and are adaptable to any grade level. They can be incorporated into lessons on related topics or used to introduce/involve students in the Liturgy of the Word. Includes stage directions, background notes, discussion questions, and a prayer activity.

144 pp, $14.95 (order J-25)

Acting Out the Miracles and Parables
52 Five-Minute Plays for Education and Worship
Mary Kathleen Glavich, SND

These 52 playlets, adaptable for all grades, will enliven and enrich religion classes and "do learning" in a way that students will remember.

144 pp, $12.95 (order W-64)

Easiest Gospel Plays Ever
Trudy Schommer

Students (ages 7 to 11) can use creativity and their own dialogue to bring these stories to life. Includes directions for setting the stage, patterns, and directions for suggested props or costumes.

56 pp, $7.95 (W-62)

Leading Students into Scripture
Mary Kathleen Glavich, SND

Sr. Kathleen offers creative suggestions for helping children (pre-K and up) learn about and personalize the scriptural messages. Includes rewriting Scripture prayers, memorizing Scripture, creating scriptural art, playing Bible games, and much, much more.

144 pp, $12.95 (order W-18)

Jesus for Children
William Griffin

The life of Jesus is faithfully retold from Scripture in contemporary language, in over fifty read-aloud stories for young children (ages 6 to 9). Presents the events of Jesus' life from a child's-eye view.

144 pp, $9.95 (order M-05)

Available at religious bookstores or from:

XXIII

TWENTY-THIRD PUBLICATIONS

P.O. BOX 180 • 185 WILLOW ST. • MYSTIC, CT 06355 • 1-860-536-2611 • 1-800-321-0411 • FAX 1-800-572-0788

Call for a free catalog